From the Teacher's Closet

AUTHORIZED EDITION

Wayne R. Siligo

ISBN-13: 9781086460131

Edited by Christina Ge

Dedication

This book is dedicated to my daughter, Julie Page.
In her twenty-six years, she gave those around her a century of joy.

Table of Contents:

About the Author:

Wayne Siligo, a San Francisco Bay Area professional musician, is also an award-winning Special Education teacher and Director of Music at The California School for the Blind in Fremont, California. He lives with his wife, Janet, on Alameda Island in the San Francisco Bay.

His latest work, "From the Teacher's Closet," is a compelling collection of humorous and bizarre life experiences. The reader will not only curl up into similar memories and emotions but be drawn into his fascinating "Believe It or Not" personal journey. The book contains his unexpected revelation: learning of his childhood kidnapping, allowing you inside a mind-blowing introduction to his new life.

His story refuses sympathy and laughs from the gut at "character-building challenges." One thing is certain, as the story unfolds and his vision fails, each page will make you smile, outright laugh, or shake your head in either amazement or understanding empathy.

Why read a book about some character you've never heard of? I have wanted to share my experience with the millions of people in our country who are losing their sight from the gift of longevity; however, to any reader who loves a good story, I know the events in the book will give you a new and meaningful perspective on your own struggles and successes, which in itself is reason to enjoy the read.

Introduction

Kidnapped at age two and a half, I didn't know who I was or where I came from, but I soon learned, life's a never-ending gift you can't take back! All along this fantastic journey, I've lived through thousands of situations, not only flat out laughable, but often introspective and revealing of those on both sides of the experience. It angers me how in recent years, much of what the public hears about the disabled is from the adversarial viewpoint. Of course, many old stereotypes need to change, but there's another less obvious side of life with physical challenges that shouts to be told. "LAUGH AT IT, YOU'RE STILL A WINNER!" Look at your own life, even for the able-bodied guy who might be seven-foot-tall and bullet proof, everyday living is often a major challenge, and it's not always easy to take the time to look at the other guy's struggles. But it sure gets easier if we just pick up the pieces, grit our teeth, and flat out grin!

This book reveals the entertaining and humorous side of living with a disability, and gives you, the sighted reader, some understanding of the awkward situations encountered by the blind. The following narratives are informative, and many are filled with useful information. However, they are also intended to connect with you and make you smile. Through the week as I teach, travel, and play music, I short-hop questions from curious adults and kids: "What's it like to be blind?"; "How in blazes do you teach your students?" Often during these encounters, people I meet are reluctant to use the term "blind". When this happens, I always smile and say, "The terms 'visually impaired' or 'visually challenged' are great modern terms in some settings, but I think I'd rather use them to describe someone driving a car with a dirty windshield. I'm blind. And I'll bet that boo-coo cold stuff in Antarctica is still called ice." You get the drift.

Usually I try to get humor in the conversation, while making the exchange as informative as possible. Everyone, disabled or not, has special gifts waiting to be shared with others. The only requirements to be a recipient are to have an open mind and the ability to smile.

When I first began writing, I decided to present the stories in this book chronologically. Our adult adventures may be filled with more zesty herbs and spices, but our early innocence was a fertile field waiting to be planted.

1. Early Lessons—Think about it!

From first learning to tie my shoes, I knew something might be different about my vision. I didn't see the stars in the sky that seemed breathtaking to others or objects in the twilight pointed out to me as the family motored along the craggy cliffs and inlets of the Northern Pacific Coast. Many times, back home, I would leave things on the floor, and in the dark, someone would tell me to pick them up. How could they see them when I couldn't? These and dozens of other passing clues left me confused but never kept me out of trouble.

The folks I thought were my parents owned a resort lodge and boarding house near the mouth of the Klamath River in Northern California. Floyd, the husband of the couple, gave me a huge weekly allowance for helping with the housekeeping around the place, and though only seven, every weekend I'd treat some of my Native American friends from the nearby Hoopa reservation to the Saturday matinee at the old downtown theater. I had no way of knowing how poor my sight really was, for while I was able to follow some of the action on the screen, why couldn't I spot my friends in the darkened theater like everyone else?

Fortunately, losing my sight over a stretch of years allowed me time to adjust. I didn't know what normal vision was, and often managed to get into some dangerous, hilarious, and embarrassing situations (many are described later). Understand, these unusual occurrences are certainly not unique to the blind, for many with disabilities learn to work with and around them daily. It is amazing how the human mind and body adapts to changes, often fooling itself. These predicaments I jumped into were great learning experiences. Even so, as a kid many times, due to my poor sight, I would hug one of my toys and cry in bed after doing something monumentally lame or embarrassing that day. Looking back now, it may seem odd to some, but I wouldn't change a moment. Those encounters and experiences revolving around people have lit up this journey. Learning to laugh at the occasional misunderstanding of others and my own mistakes has been invaluable.

I soon realized my shins would forever appear as though they'd been tromped on by a drunken cast of "River Dance". For with uncanny accuracy, I always managed to crash into the sharpest-edged coffee table or another immovable object in the room. I was probably the only kid in Northern California, whose family bought iodine and Band-Aids at a quantity discount. Do you remember this game? In grammar school, my worst nightmare was the diabolical skirmish named dodge or "splatter" ball, at one time played by every elementary school kid in the U.S. I'm sure the credos game was invented a hundred years ago by some frustrated teacher who finally found a legal way to get even with his unruly charges. I can visualize him rubbing his hands together while doing a little dance, all the while smiling evilly at his over-active lunch toters' plight. The grin broadened each time one of his least favorite scholars caught one of those big, insidious, damned rubber balls on the side of the head. I was always too proud to admit I couldn't see and was the first to be eliminated, breaking two pair of glasses before it dawned on me to first take the worthless things off.

If you think about it, it's difficult for a youngster to know what it's like to see normally, if they've never had normal vision. They have no way to judge or compare their sight to the other kids around them. To them, what they see is what everyone else sees. Then the phenomenon works in reverse, those who see perfectly can't imagine what it's like for those who don't. Because of my rare eye disease, glasses only slightly improved my vision, but at the time, they were the only aid eye doctors thought could help. Perhaps a thousand times, after one of my blunders or accidents, someone has said, "Hey, jackass! Why don't you get some better glasses?" I often wanted to say, "Well, oh wizened one, I will, as soon as you get some better brains!"

One of the most refreshing traits of youth is the curiosity and the "I want to do it" attitude. When we're young, thank God we haven't yet learned to apply future acquired limitations on our creativity and natural talents. This curiosity and "jump into it up to my nose" trait got me in some interesting situations, and I'll admit it up front, I loved every minute of it. To this day I like to cook but was a miserable failure at desserts from the beginning, as you'll soon see.

2. One Cook Too Many in the Kitchen

There were numerous logging camps and lumber mills in the Coastal Mountains along the Klamath River. For two years, as they built their resort, my folks ran a popular boarding house for the lumbermen and loggers working in the camps. Every morning before dawn, I'd get up and help my stepmom Anne, in the kitchen. She served the twenty-five or so men staying with us three meals a day. I'd help her put bag lunches together each morning after she let me light the old Wedgewood wood-burning stove. We boarded an interesting mixture of men at the place: Poles, Swedes, Italians, and an occasional Irishman thrown in for a spontaneous tear-jerking song. One of the Swedes' favorite dishes was a concoction they had to have at breakfast, or they refused to leave for work: "Uts," or something sounding like that. This nutritious "heart-healthy" repast was built by frying a few quarts of salted raw oats in a huge iron skillet in an inch of bacon grease — "Numm, Numm."

We were so far from the nearest town. Often Mrs. Cummings, the retired bookkeeper from the lumber mill, would come up to the boarding house and keep an eye on me while the folks took the snaking two-hour drive north on Highway 1 to Crescent City, the closest town of any size. Mrs. Cummings was a little stout woman, good-natured and really neat (she let me do nearly anything I wanted). She usually reclined in the front room, smoking Chesterfields and nipping from the brandy bottle she managed to sneak in every Saturday in her sewing bag.

One weekend, shortly after arriving, I heard her snoring loudly in Floyd's leather chair, so I decided it was time to try my skill at cooking from scratch. In the kitchen I dragged out one of Anne's huge cookbooks, and with my nose an inch from the pages, tried to find her recipe for

15

peach dumplings. But the print was faded and too small for me to read, and besides, I'd been with her dozens of times before when she'd made them. I knew most of the ingredients and the general way they went together. So, I decided to use the "wing it from memory" technique. Julia Child, rest her glorious soul, would have been proud!

No joke intended, the dumplings were a piece of cake: a monster gulumpa of Bisquick; a smaller gulumpa of buttermilk; a half a smaller gulumpa of sugar; a smattering gulumpa of oil; then, an important tiny hiccup gulumpa of salt— voila!

From the pantry, I had lugged out four one-quart Mason jars of home canned peaches. I'd helped Anne can them the summer before. Of course, it had not yet dawned on my industrious mind that I was making enough dumplings to feed the Dallas Cowboys. I found the huge pot Anne used to boil large things, but it was too heavy for me. I soon found a shallower pot, pouring in a few inches of water. It seemed the fastest and least messy technique to heat the peaches was to leave them in the shallow pan on the stove in their sealed jars, then later plop the dumplings into a bowl with them, after they'd warmed up. Pleased with the overall result of my gastronomic labors, I headed for the front room to listen to my favorite cartoon show, just starting: "Here He Comes to Save the Day!" I'd completely forgotten about my clandestine dessert when a shattering explosion came from the kitchen. Anne's Boston Bull Terrier, Spooky, lived up to his dumb name dismissing my protection by retreating post-haste under the couch. Immediately, the other three jars exploded after the first. Mrs. Cummings jumped awake, emitting language having something to do with bathroom bodily functions. I was confused as I ran in the kitchen behind her. Of course, the peach jars had exploded on the stove, scattering peaches and splintered glass in all directions. The sticky fruit in its heavy, sweet syrup drooped from utensils and fixtures on the walls. Halves of the fruit were plastered on the ceiling, windows, and cabinets. I heard from Anne later that the most interesting sight was the grenade-like pieces of fruit that'd hit the screen over the kitchen sink. She said the fruit had been strained nearly halfway through the mesh of the screen.

I felt sorry for poor Mrs. Cummings, because all the time we were trying to clean up the mess before the folks got home, she kept saying something about God helping her, and I knew that even with his unlimited resources, we wouldn't be finished in time. For the next year I was barred from further culinary masterpieces and was given an intensive crash course in general physics, something about the sum pressure of boiling peach juice in a vacuum, and the surface tension of leather belt applied to jean-sheathed butt. Sadly, my Saturday sidekick was rudely dismissed, and often I wondered if her memory of the dumpling fiasco was sour enough for her to give up the sauce. It dawned on me later that perhaps it had the reverse effect.

3. Santa was a Fisherman

So vividly I remember a rust streaked seven story incinerator that loomed just south of our resort property on northern California Coast Highway One. It stood next to the lumber mill, and its towering shape had always seemed sinister to me, a lurking ghost I could never forget. Yet, I still remember a more terrifying image. It was framed by a stormy morning as I stared in disbelief from the back porch of our huge two-story home.

As I squinted through the driving rain, I felt a mixture of raw fear and fascination. The Klamath River, which flowed two hundred yards south, had changed its course during the storm last night. Now the muddy water roiled and tumbled just a few feet from the back porch. In the distance, silhouetted against the bleak morning sky, the mill's incinerator began to move, slowly turning on its concrete base. Screeching, it tipped over onto its side and began rolling. I witnessed the water's power as the huge burner tumbled down river, as if it were an angry Goliath's discarded toy. The wind shrieked at gale-force, and I watched with a child's innocent sadness as the bodies of drowned farm animals floated past. It was only a whimpering beginning. Out of the area on business, the folks had left me in the care of Mrs. Cunningham and were unable to return. Within hours of the onslaught of the storm, all the river's bridges had been torn away.

Around midnight on the second night of the flood, the rising torrent began forcing our house to rotate on its foundation. Near one A.M., we heard yelling outside in the wind. We directed a flashlight out into the darkness off the back porch, and then shouted in joy and relief. We recognized the familiar figure of our family friend, old Cyrus Keating, standing at the bow of his aging twenty-five-foot salmon boat. His grey bearded round face was dripping wet from the storm. Floyd stood behind him at the helm. Just an hour after they rescued us, in piles of shattered wreckage, our trailer park, the boardinghouse, our fifteen-cabin motel, and the huge Victorian house that had been my imaginary castle, were swept down the river into the Pacific Ocean. I remember the scream of the boat's big engine as we fought our way back upstream through the half-frozen rain. Floyd shivered violently from the cold. Years later I realize his trembling was not only from the bitter wind, but also a reaction to the fear of what the future held for our family. Wrapped in old Cyrus's thick sea coat, I could never forget the strange mixture of smells whenever the gentle old man hugged me. There was the ever-present nutty scent of Union Leader pipe tobacco mixed with Old Spice aftershave along with the pungent smell of salmon eggs. Add to these, the odor of his musty shirt, often in need of laundering, and on occasion the strong, but not unpleasant, hint of Old Grand Dad bourbon. From that raging night on, we knew Cy had saved our lives. Out of her mind with worry, Anne was waiting for us at the last road still open south.

The following few years were a study in despair and frustration for our small family. Floyd managed to rent a tiny dilapidated house along the railroad tracks near McKinleyville, California; we soon realized we were in a state of poverty that we had never experienced. Cy's precious gifts of smoked and frozen salmon arrived by delivery every few weeks, giving us a break from beans and cheap hamburgers. Floyd worked two jobs, while Anne worked long shifts in a nearby café. I understood our predicament but hated being called "the kid from the old shack house who never has any money."

Not long after beginning school, students were told to bring tennis shoes for outside activities. My folks couldn't afford a new pair, so Anne found some sneakers at a secondhand store. They were two sizes too big and particularly wide across the toes. When I ran, they noisily slapped on the ground, making the dust puff out around my feet. In one day, I had three fights and had been nicknamed, "Bozo the Clown Feet." I never complained, because I knew Floyd had been wearing secondhand boots to work for months.

When Christmas approached that year, I had some fantasy wishes on my Santa list. First was a bicycle, but under the tree, the gifts were meager. I told Dad I was wishing for a bike from Santa. His face clouded as he placed his hands on my shoulders. Both hands were disfigured; the middle fingers of the right were fused at birth, and the index of his left had been severed in the Army by an exploding hydraulic hose. He squeezed those rough but magic hands and told me, "Wayne, in life, we don't often get exactly what we want, but there's always a good reason." Of course, on Christmas morning there was no bicycle, but there was a handmade sweater and some new socks. Anne gave me a World Atlas that I used until I lost nearly all my remaining vision in my twenties. I'd suspected Santa didn't exist, but, secretly, I wanted to be wrong. Confused emotions clouded my thoughts. I wanted everything to be the way it had been, those rich, warm Christmases before, when Santa was as real as the old rusty incinerator at the mill down the road.

Around noon Christmas Day, while playing in the yard, I saw a truck approaching on the gravel path beside the tracks. I stood up and recognized the dusty black paint of Cyrus Keating's battered Chevy pickup. As he rolled to a stop, I began running. Dad came out of the house, surprised to see who had arrived. Old Cyrus got out and walked to the rear of the truck. He lifted out a shiny new Schwinn Custom Cruiser bicycle then laughed, "Santa left this with me. He said he was sorry, but he didn't have your new address. I told him I knew right where you lived, and I'd be glad to deliver it for him." I was squealing with joy while I fought back tears. I ran back and forth, torn between wanting to touch the bike and hug Cyrus at the same time. When I looked at Dad, there was no mistaking the tears in his eyes. I rode that bicycle for the next five years until it was stolen. I've often wondered how many thousands of miles I traveled on it and how many newspapers I delivered.

I cried openly for hours when Cyrus died during my freshman year of high school. Though he was no longer with us, we could never forget his gifts to our family: gifts of life and joy to all of us, and especially to a thankful boy who to this day still believes in the gift of giving and the spirit of Santa. I've worn Old Spice cologne since I started shaving in my teens. Often old memories come to mind when I smell the scent of unsweetened pipe tobacco, smoked salmon, or the occasional whiff of a good Kentucky Bourbon whiskey.

4. Hi! Have a Tamale?

Over a decade after the movie *The African Queen* was released, the local drive-in movie showed a series of classic films. At the time, the drive-in was a new and fun venue for everyone. The entire family could go see a flick for a few bucks. Dads could kick off their shoes and down an occasional brew from the trunk, and moms could wear casual clothes and forget about make-up for a change. We had our own favorite parking space and always arrived early to beat anyone to it.

At the beginning of a film, Floyd would often send me to the snack bar for some eats. Since we always arrived before dark, I had the position of the snack-shack memorized. When I left the car after dark to head to the snack-shack, I'd touch gently and count each car in our row down to the walkway in the center of the drive-in. Then, I'd walk down the center aisle towards the bright lights of the snack bar, carefully counting the rows I passed along the way. It was easy for I could hear the sound of the portable speakers hanging from the windows of the cars on each aisle. After loading up a tray with popcorn, cokes, and four steaming red-hot tamales, I'd head back to the car.

At that very moment, bullets were flying, and Bogie was struggling with the aging steam engine on the boat while Katharine Hepburn tried desperately to steer the Queen down the rapids. I could clearly hear the dialogue on the screen through the speakers on the cars I passed and couldn't help staring at the screen in front of me. Turning left, I counted the cars down the aisle until I reached our "new" used Pontiac. Bogie was screaming at Katharine to hold the tiller straight as I opened the back door and climbed in. When I looked ahead, I thought the windshield seemed a little steamed up. My backside had barely hit the seat when I heard a scream that would have further deafened Quasimodo! I jumped straight up, slamming my head on the roof of the car, dumping the entire contents of the tray in the back seat. I heard a strange, gruff male voice from behind the steering wheel curse, bellowing in my direction. I don't remember getting out of the car, but Floyd appeared in his stocking feet, trying to explain to the angry lovers that I'd climbed into the wrong car. I do remember Floyd giving the guy some money to help pay for cleaning his upholstery. It sounds so stupid now, but after the humiliation of the moment, later that night I wondered if the couple ever ate the tamales. It was years later before I found out if Katherine steered the boat all the way down the rapids without Bogie's help.

5. Lost at Sea

One sweltering summer a year or so later, we visited distant relatives in Oklahoma. They took us to a large lake on the Texas border for a weekend of "bah-bee-coos" and hoedowns. On the second day after lunch, I sat on the edge of the lake listening to my very pretty cousin talk. I've always loved southern folks' accents. It's fascinating, the word "tire." (They pronounce it "tar".) It's a "fits all" word, describing the tower on the hill, the flat on the car. Put a "d" on the end of it, and you're really pooped, or very overheated, waiting to be feathered.

In her fascinating drawl she described the features of the large lake and the train trestle crossing it a half mile across the water. I've always been a strong swimmer, but to this day I don't know why I decided to do what follows. I guess I was showing off to the young girl. My description of what follows is still vivid. For years I had frequent nightmares, reliving it over and over again.

The next thing I knew I was swimming in the direction of the train trestle. The water was warm and smooth, and I covered the distance quickly. I remembered a lot of glare off the water and not being able to see the trestle clearly in the distance, but thought I was seeing a shape of some kind ahead. After a few more minutes I was close enough to make out the dark pilings under the trestle. Moments later, I grabbed the moss-covered structures supporting the railroad bridge. I was proud and felt only slightly fatigued. I remember hanging onto the slimy piling for some time, gathering breath for the trip back to the beach. I decided to breaststroke for a while, so later, when I was closer to the shoreline, it would be easier to see the dock.

Rolling over on my back allowed me to make out a large group of low thunderheads beginning to fill the sky. In only minutes everything had darkened, and I quickly learned about sudden Southern thunderstorms! Swimming faster and feeling a surge of adrenalin, I soon found that instead of giving me added energy, it only seemed to slow me down and sap my strength. The once placid water began to chop and roll as the oncoming wind agitated the lake's surface. The rising waves began to fill my mouth, forcing me to return to free-style. Stopping to look ahead, I felt a last surge of adrenaline envelop me. Nothing was visible in any direction. Huge raindrops drove down onto the surface, stirring up the water into a misty mixture of evaporation and rain. I knew at that moment I had no idea in what direction I was swimming. Having no visual points of reference made me certain I'd changed course.

As clear as yesterday, I recall the lightning shooting across the sky and the shock waves of the booming thunder as it bounced off the roiling water. Then the terror I experienced earlier multiplied tenfold. I felt the hamstring muscle of my right leg begin to tighten. Trying desperately to relax only seemed to make it worse. Feeling the strength leaving me in a way I'd never felt before, the terror pressed even closer in my chest. Rolling over again I tried to backstroke, but the rain was coming down too hard to breathe with my mouth open. It is possible that I screamed out loud as the hamstring of my other leg cramped hard without warning. Then, the old saying about not swimming after eating echoed in my head. Somewhere in the distance I thought I heard the sound of a motor, but the roar of the driving rain on the water disguised it.

It became more difficult to keep my mouth above water, and at that moment, for the first time, the cold realization hit me— I was going to drown. Through my fear, I heard the engine sound again, this time coming closer. I knew then that it was an outboard motor. Then the thought raced through my mind: "What if they run over me?" They surely can't see me in this rain. The boat passed slowly somewhere a few yards off to my left, but as I tried to yell to them, the screams choked in my throat, and in seconds the boat was gone.

It's impossible to know now how long I struggled to keep my head above water, but it seemed like hours. Then, as suddenly as it had rolled in, the storm blew past and the heat of the sun was on my head and shoulders. Turning belly-over, I dragged my nearly useless legs behind me, and to my amazement saw the blurry shape of the boat dock and the beach not more than a few hundred feet off to my right. Minutes later, as I again heard the outboard behind me, I began to crawl up onto the steep bank. The scraping gravel and rocks on my bloody embows and knees couldn't have felt better. Relieved and ashamed, the tears wouldn't stop.

An older woman came over to me and asked if I was all right. And then came the shrill voice of Anne. My cousin had gone back to the cabin to get her, and when I didn't return, they'd sent the dock crew out looking for me. I learned some lasting and valuable lessons that day. One, don't climb down the well unless you can damn sure climb back out. Two, frantic woman's compassionate mood can radically change once she sees your butt is safe. And three, the most memorable lesson: don't attempt to sit on a hard surface for at least three days after a bonding experience with some of Anne Mae's hand-picked willow switches!

6. Over the Meadow and Through the Woods

Very early on, those with vision impairments learn to depend on the help and feedback of others. Of course, this requires a lot of trust from those with the poor vision. Early, I learned not to always believe the description of a situation, until checking a few things out myself. It may have been my misfortune, but most of my friends were a few years older. In some ways it was great, for they taught me a lot about the real world, and probably more than I needed to know about some things. Still, it seemed that hanging around with the older guys always led to trouble. A half-mile from our home in the Coastal Mountains was a steep rising area known as Old Lookout Hill, a hangout for some of the budding delinquents. Secluded and high up the mountain, it was a perfect spot to smoke an occasional stolen cigarette or sneak a peek at some girlie magazine carefully "borrowed" from someone's uncle or dad. On rare occasions, someone would bring a couple of beers or a partially filled bottle of Port or Chablis wine. Of course, you realize that I would never have tried any of these vices if those "bully" older friends of mine hadn't insisted!

Lazy and bored one hot summer afternoon, the gang was laying around telling well-worn dirty jokes in the shade of a large Scrub Oak. Daring us to try something, one of the boys came up with a hare-brained idea. On top of the hill a few yards away sat a rusting hulk of a large truck chassis. The cab had been removed years before, and all that remained was the bed, the heavy frame, the stripped engine block, the seat, and the steering assembly. All four large wheels were still attached, but of course the tires were flat and rotten. Someone suggested we rock the old wreck back and forth, get it rolling downhill, then jump on for a ride.

A one-lane road ran across the base of the hill a few hundred yards below, and we could ride it on down to the flat ground leading to a bridge over the creek. Rudy, the oldest and biggest of the gang, told me not to worry for the hill wasn't too steep. Now I know I must've been out of my mind, but like the rest at the time, I thought he had a killer idea. The six of us cleared the junk from in front of the hulk and went to work trying to get it to move forward. Because of the slight downhill slope, we were surprised how easily it moved once we broke the wheels free from the weeds and mud where it had been sitting for years. The old wreck began rolling off the sloping ground and on down the hill. Teasing and setting me up, one of the guys yelled for me to steer.

I jumped into the tattered remains of the driver's seat as the other boys hopped onto the rotten rear bed for the coming ride. I remember the terror and electric-like shock in my stomach when I discovered that the steering wheel, frozen rigid with rust for years, had now suddenly broken loose and was useless. None of us had bothered to check to see if the tie rods and steering assembly were connected! The front axle seemed frozen, the wheels pointing straight ahead. Once the old truck began to accelerate, the steering wheel spun in my hands like a lazy Susan. Some of the boys began yelling as the chassis gained speed, and we soon realized we'd made a serious miscalculation of the angle of the hill and the speed of the old wreck. We were soon bouncing and rattling at an alarming speed down the bumpy, steep hillside. I remember being thankful there were no trees in our path. Then I became aware of some of the guys jumping off, responding to someone's cry to abandon ship. By now I held the wheel in a grip of fear and self-preservation, for the thing was bouncing too much for me to get out from behind the wheel. The outcroppings of bedrock and small boulders halfway down the side of the hill convinced me to stay put. Pieces of rotten rubber and sparks kept flying off the front wheels, and I heard the shriek of the steel rims as they raced over the flat pieces of bedrock jutting out of the steep hillside. My vision was so poor I couldn't see the road they'd talked about ahead. I had no idea what was waiting on the other side of it. The next few seconds were a blur of noises and flashing movement. The old wreck bounced over a small gully along the side of the dirt road and flew across to the other side. Coming close to being thrown off, only my death grip on the steering wheel saved me from serious injury. I do remember the sound of metal pieces flying off the wreck.

Still rolling very fast, I started down another slope on the opposite side of the road. I recall careening through someone's vegetable garden, and green things flying in different directions. Then to add to my predicament, directly ahead was a high wooden slat fence, painted as white as my skinny knuckles on the cracked steering wheel. How I made it through the fence without serious cuts or injuries is a miracle, but it only slightly slowed me down. I opened my eyes, and instantly wished I hadn't, for dead ahead on the still sloping ground stood a large, square laundry line setup filled with drying clothes! The right side of the wreck caught the aluminum pole in the center of the carousel and clipped it off with simplistic efficiency. Still the heavy chassis rolled forward, but now I felt it was finally slowing down, as the metal wheel rims of my wayward steed cut into the soft grass of the home's huge backyard.

I know I must've groaned aloud, for just a few feet ahead sat an old-fashioned ornamental brick well. The old wreck crashed into it with enough force to cause considerable damage to its brickwork and tiles, and the jamming of the steering wheel into my chest as I flew forward left a deep bruise that remained for a month. I was lucky to come through the entire fiasco with only a few deep scratches and bruises.

Over the next few days, after a most unpleasant "attitude adjustment" from Floyd, I was again reminded of the necessity of being able to sit, when nature's call could no longer be ignored. Floyd paid for the neighbor's damage, doing most of the repairs himself, but it took me nearly six months of emptying trash and stacking wood to repay him for the materials to complete the repairs. It's a good idea to check your parachute before you jump out of the plane, or just maybe you should forget the credos idea in the first place. Another lesson learned.

7. Believe me— I didn't see it!

Having lost the resort in that devastating flood that changed the course of the river, we moved just north of the San Francisco Bay Area and struggled along for the next few years. With the folks' hard work and dedication, we gradually got back on our feet financially. My freshman year of high school, Floyd went to work as a partner with a growing construction company. He traveled to Northern California to begin a job building a small two-lane road through the mountains east of Willow Creek on the Coastal Range. When school finished in June that year, Anne and I locked the house and headed north to join him. Though the landscape there was rugged and beautiful, the heat was oppressive and the paths and gullies up and down the creek were crawling with rattlesnakes. The squadrons of mosquitoes that came out at night would literally chase anyone inside if they weren't covered from head to toe.

We lived in a twenty-foot house trailer, a bit dilapidated, but the roof didn't leak. The first time I went to the creek for water, the rattlesnakes emphatically convinced me that maybe water wasn't such an urgent priority after all. Floyd took a .22 zipper rifle and spent the next hour and a half reducing the viper population. It didn't take me long to learn where all the crawly critters' favorite hiding places were, and I always gave any bush or fallen log (where there might be some shade) a wide berth during the heat of the day. One of my fondest memories of that summer, is the wonderful sounds of the night. We were a ninety minutes' drive from any town or major highway so I could hear for miles.

The only sound that interrupted the others of the night was the rare drone of an airplane passing somewhere in the distance. At times it was so quiet I heard squirrels and other small mammals scurrying around in the trees dozens of yards away. Sitting with netting over my neck and face, I'd listen to the deer and other larger animals come to the creek side to drink. As long as I stayed downwind and was still, they rarely noticed me. It's hard to explain, but even though I couldn't see them, just being near those animals gave me a feeling of peace and awe.

We stayed there for almost three months, and I had every path, obstacle and hanging branch memorized. Most of the bigger immovable objects along the paths had long before been painfully introduced to my shins or other body parts. As the summer waned, the job began to fall behind schedule, and Floyd started working later in the evening with the crew using gas-powered generators for light. Often he wouldn't get home 'til well after midnight.

One unforgettable evening, Anne sent me down to the creek to fill two large buckets with water. I could have walked the path backward; I'd been down it so many times. As I climbed down the last few feet of the slope leading to the creek's edge, I heard a sound that sent a shock of terror through me so hard it nearly knocked me down. The sound was deep and guttural, almost human, but so low and powerful I felt my insides shake from its vibration. I remember losing my footing and falling backward, making a futile attempt at placing both water buckets in low Earth orbit. At the same moment, whatever was near began moving quickly, thankfully away from me. I swear I felt the ground shake from the animal's weight, and over the sound of the running water, I heard the snap of breaking branches and limbs. I sat still for the longest time, trying to get my heart unjammed from my throat.

That night was the only time in my life that I remember being so scared I wet my pants. I was shaking so much I could barely walk. Retrieving the water buckets early the next morning, I knew there was no way on Earth— Anne's switches included— that I was going down to that creek again at night. Of course, the neighbors on the crew said I had surprised a bear. I had been raised along the Klamath River and had seen bears for years, sometimes watching them fight during mating season. The sound I heard that night was absolutely nothing like any bear I'd ever heard. If that animal was a bear, he'd been taking World Wrestling Association roaring classes along with frequent steroid and testosterone injections! I never truly believed in the fantastic stories about the Sasquatch or "Big Foot," described by the local Indians and old-timers of that area and had always thought the whole thing was a crock of overblown folklore. But after that night at the creek and what happened a few weeks later, I've always left the door to my disbelief open just a crack.

At the beginning of the month, the road crew locked up the heavy equipment and service vehicles in the fenced-in service yard they'd built a few miles up the road. It was July Fourth weekend, and the boss had decided to give the crew a few days off for a well-deserved rest. The following morning one of the construction bosses drove up in a hurry, leaving his truck running as he pounded on our trailer door. Floyd got out of bed, as the foreman explained sometime during the previous night, someone had broken into the yard and destroyed a lot of supplies and equipment. Floyd and I threw on some clothes and jumped in the truck, heading up the newly built road. When we arrived at the site, we couldn't believe the damage to the service yard! Full 55-gallon drums of diesel fuel were strewn all over, some ruptured and empty, others dented badly. Floyd said later the strange thing about the drums was that they'd been thrown uphill from where they'd been stored. The corrugated storage shed was torn open and some of the two-by-four supports had been broken like matchsticks. Spare equipment parts and air filters were scattered in every direction. The cyclone fencing on the south side of the compound had been ripped open as if it had been cheesecloth. There were no clear footprints because the yard had been built on a large outcropping of bedrock for safety and ease of access during the sudden coastal rains. I do remember that a few large smudges were found on the rock from whoever (or whatever) stepped in some of the spilled oil.

The police arrived later that day and investigated but couldn't explain everything they found. I remember Floyd saying there were several large chunks torn from the surface of the rocks from the edges of the full drums striking the bedrock. This would indicate that they had been dropped or physically thrown. I knew how much one of those drums weighed, having moved them with a heavy dolly while helping Floyd load the service and grease truck. Bears don't have an opposable thumb, so it is extremely difficult for them to pick up objects above their heads or grasp them to throw forward. They almost always swipe at objects and encircle things with their paws or press things against their bodies to carry them. The most interesting observation from the break-in was the total lack of claw marks on any building surfaces or on any of the damaged equipment.

In past decades, the Sasquatch phenomenon has faded into oblivion, and I don't know what I ran into that night. But somehow, I wonder if my poor eyesight has enhanced the mental image of what was there. Just maybe, the old Indians who still believe in the huge Sasquatch would say my night-blindness might have been a blessing in disguise.

8. Double Jeopardy

Now that I'd started high school, I thought it was a good plan to go out and find a real job, one where the boss told me where to go, paid me by the hour, and told me what to do. I wanted something more challenging than delivering newspapers and knocking on doors trying to collect or sell subscriptions (I had no idea this very knocking on doors would make me a very well-moneyed young man in the near future).

Those were fabulous times, for if a kid wanted a job, all he or she had to do was go out and make the rounds, banging on doors asking the business owners if they wanted any help. We weren't yet aware of the scary worries of child abuse, sexual harassment, exploitation of minors, or over exposure to lead-based paint or Radon. I thought it was about time to get out in the "real" world and find a "real" job.

My first few weekends of searching were a total bust, finding only "weed pulling" gigs and "babysitting" of outside inventory and equipment, or an occasional delivery of flyers about upcoming sales for various stores. This wouldn't do for an aspiring financial mogul such as myself. It was too much like delivering newspapers. At least with delivering the daily news, once a month, I was treated to seeing a pretty mom, or if I was really lucky, her daughter, open the door when I came around collecting.

I must digress for a moment, for this last phenomenon deserves a little recognition. You wouldn't believe some of the things that came down while I was waiting at the door for someone to pay me. Once a poor, harried woman who must have just jumped out of the shower, answered the door with a bathrobe thrown over her shoulders. She was not at all happy to see my broad smile and bright, cheery delivery of, "Good afternoon ma'am, collecting for the Daily Review." She opened the door about sixteen inches and in her bare feet reached out to take the small ticket receipt I pushed in her direction. I'd learned very early, if you gave subscribers the receipt before they paid, they would somehow find the money and wouldn't put you off 'til the next week or so. I noticed the sleeve of her bathrobe hanging down her arm as she was hiding behind the door. I knew she wasn't ready to accept an Oscar for "most dynamic dresser of local suburbs." When she turned to go somewhere in the house to get my money, the sleeve or belt of her bathrobe must have caught on the doorknob or something on the back of the door As she turned and moved quickly away, the entire terrycloth robe decided to obey gravity and head earthward. I couldn't see very well, but there was no way I could have missed that Rubenesque sight, especially because the front drapes were open, and the sun was behind me. Standing in the center of the front room as naked as a Playboy model, the poor lady screamed and boogied back behind the door. I was rudely dismissed and was told to come back in a few days (She kept the receipt!).

On another occasion fairly late in the evening, (a good time to collect, because people were home by then) another housewife answered the door, (remember this was more than a few decades ago) a cigarette dangled from the corner of her mouth and her hair was hanging down her forehead in stringy strands. Even with my poor vision, I saw she was perspiring freely. She was obviously in the middle of some task. In the background I heard the splash of water and kids arguing. She was about to open her mouth to ask what I wanted when a high-piercing child's scream came from the direction of the splashing water, "Mom! MOM! Come here quick! Billy's standing up and peeing in the tub!"

I have to confess I was courteous and could take my share of abuse most of the time, but there was one subscriber who didn't like me, and I didn't like him much either. He smoked huge cigars, and I rarely saw him without a beer in his hand. He was the spitting image of Archie Bunker from *All in the Family* on a bad night. One rainy evening, I was wet and cold and needed to go to the bathroom. I had at least two hours of homework still waiting at home. As I walked up this guy's steps to his front door to collect for the paper, I swear I saw him get up from his chair next to the front window. Before I could knock, the door opened abruptly and "Sweetness," enveloping me in a cloud of stinking smoke, roared, "We don't want any!" The devil made me do it. I immediately quipped, "any WHAT?" "Oh well," I thought later, after my ears stopped ringing from the slamming door, "He wasn't that great a customer after all."

33

As I mentioned, looking for a new job was a decided challenge. After some weeks of searching I finally got my first big break. For three weeks, I'd been hustling a job from a Japanese gardener who ran a very successful nursery near the Nimitz Freeway a few miles from home. The hard-working man finally gave in and said in his very hard to understand English he would give me a try but would give no pay until he saw my work. I had absolutely no experience with plants, shrubs, seeds, or fertilizers. My idea of a plant was an avocado seed, toothpicks sticking in it, suspended in a glass of water on the windowsill above the kitchen sink! Heck, I was such an expert on botany, on a good night, I could identify at least half the chopped-up things in my salad.

The first thing he told me to do was to open a big wire-meshed iron gate and water a huge bunch of potted plants behind it. Nervous and eager to please, I hustled over to the gate and set to opening it. The damn thing had a cast-iron latch on it that must have been designed by some Shinto sorcerer from the twelfth century; I couldn't figure out how to open it. After finally deciphering the way it worked, I felt the sweat running into my eyes and my hands shaking. I also felt the stony glare of Nobue Kawabata, my prospective employer piercing the surface of my backside. As I gave the heavy gate a giant push. My hands were slippery with perspiration and it flew from my grasp. I rushed after it in horror, as the twenty-five-foot gate swung past the point where the sidewalk ended, and with an almost diabolic purpose, swung out into the plot crammed with potted greenery. It was just high enough to clear the tops of the metal containers holding the plants, and with unerring accuracy, cleanly snapped every one of the fifty or so plants off two inches above the dirt in their pots. All I remember was a shriek of Japanese profanity (at least that's what I thought it was!). It didn't take long to surmise my gig was over, and I didn't even look back as I sprinted down the street in full retreat.

— And now, the rest of the story —

A few months later I was given a larger more lucrative paper route near the Hayward airport. One of the houses where I delivered a paper every night was a beautiful corner lot with many ornamental plants and statuary around the large fenced and gated yard. The first time I tried to collect from the house, I only made it halfway down the walk from the gate to the front door when a large black Doberman greeted me from the porch having every intention of making me an evening appetizer. Not wishing to be an "In memory of" at such a young age, I made a serious attempt at the present Olympic one-hundred-yard dash world record. I was amazed at the ease I cleared the top of the gate and knew then and there I had a future as a world class hurdler. The poor Dobie hit the gate with such force it nearly knocked him unconscious. The front door opened, and a tiny Japanese woman yelled at the dog to come in the house. The animal obeyed, wobbling a little groggily as it went inside. She told me to never open the gate in the future and ring the button on the buzzer to the door right of the mailbox. I glanced over to the box and realized I hadn't checked the name on my receipts. In large black script, the box read: Nobue and Loti Kawabata. For a second, I felt like running like a mugger, but then she spoke again, "Just throw the paper up here near the porch every day, and I will find it when I come out. Thank you, young man." For the next few weeks everything went smoothly, and their paper always landed on the broad cement of their porch. I took pride in my prowess at folding and sailing papers and once I'd checked out and learned the distance, could place one from a pedaled bicycle nearly any where I wanted.

One particular Saturday afternoon, I was running late and was jamming a little faster than usual. I rounded the corner of my "ex" employer's" house. After making the turn, I reached back and down with my right hand and grabbed a folded paper from the canvas bag that straddled the rear wheel of my bike. It was one of one-hundred-forty I delivered every day. Seeing the shape of their gate on my left, I snapped my wrist, sailing the paper in the direction of the porch of the house. Casually watching the flight of the paper from the corner of my "good" eye, I nearly had a heart attack as I saw someone, back to the street, bending over, working on the front screen door. In a beautiful arc, the paper spun through the air in its majestic flight then plummeted down accurately toward the front door. I nearly crashed my bike as in disbelief. I saw the newspaper land soundly on the butt of the bending person. Caught totally off-guard and holding a screwdriver in his hand, the poor man plunged headfirst through the newly hung screen door he'd just installed. I knew I was out of a job with the paper if I just rode off, so nearly in tears, I turned around and pedaled back to the scene of the forced error. Knowing what I know now, I could have said I was impaired by the influence of steroids or suffering from ADHD or perhaps a mental condition brought on by stale Twinkies, but it was bullet-biting time. As I approached the gate on foot again my worst fears were realized. Mr. Kawabata had extricated himself from the ruined screen and was violently shaking the screwdriver in my direction exhausting the remainder of his Japanese profanity ammunition (at least that's what I thought it was!) Again, as in so many times in my life, a woman saved my tush. Mrs. Kawabata came out on the porch and convinced her irate husband to stop yelling at me. I told her I would be more than willing to pay for rescreening the new door and pleaded for her not to stop the delivery of the paper because of my foolish deed.

It was a miracle they didn't stop the paper and that the screen wire only cost me ten bucks. But I seem to remember waking up more than once in the depths of the night, sweat rolling down my face, with the memory of my dream fresh in my feverish mind. There I was, backed in a garden corner, my body much like the Jolly Green Giant's, with leaves and shrubbery growing from my person. And there, smiling diabolically, and poised on the balls of his feet was Nobue Kawabata. He was advancing slowly like an ancient Samurai warrior. His giant pruning shears snapping ominously as they waved before me!

9. A Messiah with a Crew Cut

If we are fortunate, someone in our life comes along and shakes the earth, jolting the silenced circuits enough to make us wake up and get our "show" together. As a teenager losing my eyesight, I met a man who changed my world.

My barge had broken loose and was headed out to sea. My parents were splitting up; I, a foster child who was unwanted at home, found refuge in a gang that almost took me down the shaft. Running with them had me at the door of juvenile hall on a regular basis. My grades went solidly into the flusher, and I began to embrace every vice imaginable. In the language of the time, a good description of what I had become was a "smart-mouthed punk." I'd fight anyone for the slightest reason, especially if they teased my vision, and yet, I despised what I had become. Due to the physical and mental abuse and the constant turmoil at home, I began thinking about suicide. I didn't want to live anymore. I couldn't seem to stop my "sink it to the bottom" course. I had no warning a Messiah with a crew cut was waiting in my future.

One morning, during my sophomore year of high school, I strolled into my social studies class, late as usual, but not worried in the least. By now, I was on a first name basis with the boys' dean, and in fact, we'd become almost friends. The second I entered the room, I knew something was up. It was deathly quiet.

"Well, how considerate of you to take time from your busy schedule to join us."

His sarcastic words slapped my head upright. I stared forward with my good eye, and only three feed away, saw the source of the voice. He was a muscular man of medium height wearing a dark coat and slacks with an open shirt. As he stood directly in front of me, I squinted into his piercing, steel blue eyes. It felt like the current from a stun gun was entering my scrawny body. His dark blonde hair was no more than a quarter inch long, and his nose (which must've been broken more than once) was too large for his face. I was told he had a large scar on his cheek near his right ear. While standing, he would flex the muscles of his shoulders in a way that intermittently made his coat move and jerk. I swear he looked like he'd just jumped out of the book, *Nazis I Have Known*.

He yanked over a nearby chair, placed one loafer clad foot on it, then leaned on his knee, "All of you will be proud, I'm sure, to know that your classroom antics and attitude has forced your fine counselor and teacher, Mrs. Hartley, into early retirement. Fortunately for you, I've been selected to take her place." He walked to the blackboard and in short stabbing movements, scratched his name on its surface: Ray Moore. "From this moment forward, you will address me as MISTER Moore. I've spent the last few years as a corrections officer with the Los Angeles Youth Authority, and I'll tell you now, I won't tolerate any crap from any of you! Understood?" From that day on, even the roughest dudes in class never crossed him. Attendance and completed assignments were immediately on the increase, and the class actually took on an atmosphere of learning.

Two or three weeks later, I was sitting in biology, no doubt daydreaming about a movie date with Donna, the gorgeous full-breasted blonde sitting in the row in front of me, when the P.A. crackled: "Would Roy Wayne Oliver report to Mr. Moore's office immediately after school." I felt like someone had punched me in the gut, and I'm sure I visibly began to shake. The rest of the day was a disaster. I couldn't concentrate on anything. At the three o'clock buzzer, I slid toward his office like a pig invited to a tour of Jimmy Dean Sausage Company. Mr. Moore was sitting at his desk when I knocked, and I was told to "Open It." A stack of folders lay in front of him.

"Yes sir, you wanted to see me?"

"Affirmative. Shut the door and don't bother sitting down." He thumped a finger on the folder before him and continued, "Do you know what these are?"

"No, Mister Moore" I squeaked.

"They're your test scores and aptitude tests. It's clear from these statistics what you are accomplishing right now won't cut it, not even close!" He flipped the folder closed, then put his fingertips together and stared straight in my eyes, seeming to bore into every cell of my body.

Finally, and mercifully, he spoke, "Tell me mister, who do you think you're foolin', the people who are trying to help you or yourself? You've got some big problems son and the biggest from now on is goin' to be me!" He stood up suddenly, and like a cat, was around the desk and in front of me. I remember backing up from the sheer energy of the movement. His finger pointed at my face as he spoke softly and with the most menacing tone I have ever heard, before or since. "Mister, get this straight, I'm going to be your shadow. Every time you turn around, better expect me to be watching your every move. I'm going to be in contact with your other teachers on a daily basis, and you're going to report to me every day after school. You'll finish all your assignments and turn in all your homework. No more music classes for you until the grades improve. The music teacher is behind me to the max. Monday and Thursday, soon as you can cram down your lunch, I want you in this office so we can straighten out whatever is messing up your personal life. If I can't get your parents involved and assisting me to help you, I'll find someone who can. You got all that?"

"Yes, sir," I croaked.

It seemed the following months were a fantasy journey. I began to feel good about myself. There was structure and responsibility again in my life, and I was beginning to win, win big-time. Every time I completed an assignment, Mr. Moore would go over it with me and give suggestions on how I could have improved it. He made me do a written book report on everything that I read and relate what I learned, whether it was literature or trash. Soon, he was helping me prepare lectures on World and U.S. History for me to present to our class. It didn't matter that I couldn't see so well and my problems at home were hemispheres away when I stood and presented my lesson. To this day, I'm as sure as life itself that Ray Moore is the reason I am a teacher. Every day, I can't wait to get to my school and teach. I was another of those thousands of kids that needed someone to care enough, to go that extra step to help me believe in myself.

I once heard a wonderful story. An old man was sitting in a beach chair along a stretch of pristine sand. He looked at the thousands of starfish left on the wet sand from an unusually low receding tide. Far in the distance, he saw a figure approaching. As the person came closer, he saw it was a beautiful young woman. Every few steps she'd bend down and pick up a starfish and throw it out into the lapping waves. When she came near, the old man said, "Why do you throw some of those critters back? Look how many thousands of 'em there are. What difference

10. Impossible Dream

I loved airplanes from an early age. On the weekends, I began hanging out at the Hayward airport, detailing private aircraft, and cleaning up around the flight rental agencies and the flying club while running errands and doing odd jobs. Occasionally I was rewarded with a short hop in one of my customer's planes and soon had learned some of the basics of handling aircraft controls. Of course, they would have been horrified if they knew how little I could see!

One afternoon at the airport, when the summer heat was oppressive and more humid than usual, I was yanked from my daydreaming by a sound I recognized immediately. I'd heard it dozens of times before when the crop-dusters did their work on the patchwork fields in the foothills of the central valley. Running out from under the wing of a Cessna I was waxing; I saw the familiar silhouette of a Stearman 75 Kaydet banking toward the East runway. The nimble and powerful aircraft touched down smoothly using little of the landing surface before taxiing onto the tarmac. I was excited when it came rolling in my direction. As it got close, I saw the biplane was fitted with the larger 450 HP Pratt and Whitney radial engine and its paint and detailing was magnificent. The pilot rolled the vintage beauty over to the fuel block and then dropped down from the cockpit.

I couldn't resist the chance and sprinted over to the craft hoping to ask a few questions about the Stearman. I was awed by the size of the big biplane. What followed was any young man's dream. Frank Simmons, the pilot of the Stearman was a retired Pan Am Captain and Corsair fighter pilot with the Navy during WWII. Frank was warm and casual, answering every question I shot in his direction. To my surprise, at the end of the conversation, after the fueling was finished, he asked me some magic words, "Would you like to take a hop in Lena?"

I remembered being so excited I came very close to repeating the accident in my shorts I'd accomplished after the midnight encounter with the roaring beast at the creek years earlier. In only minutes, I was strapped in the open cockpit with a headset over my ears. The following forty minutes were the shortest but most exhilarating moments of my life. On two occasions, Frank allowed me to take the duel-controlled stick, and I quickly got the feel of the responsive controls. Of course, Frank had his hands and feet on the rudder pedals and the other control stick at all times, and I soon found that without being able to see the horizon clearly, my lack of control of pitch and yaw and climb was quickly apparent. It seemed the aircraft had a natural tendency to pull to one side and climb. I had no idea what was in store after we'd made some simple turns climbs and slow banks, when Frank yelled, "Hang On!" He retook the controls and what happened next was something from the wildest carnival ride from hell or heaven. My body was upside down and backward. One moment my stomach was trying to go through the back of my torso and in the next screaming to exit my mouth. We were upside down, sideways and then without warning, I was squinting into the sun. Every few seconds my body weight tugged violently on the crossed harness, shaking my insides with every jolt. When we finally touched down, I couldn't believe I hadn't puked, but I had to hold on to Frank's shoulder in order to stand up and walk. Three more times in the following year, I was treated to a ride whenever Frank flew in from Stockton. I made sure, no matter what the family had planned, I was there!

Those magic days at the airport were just another escape vehicle for me. and deep inside, I knew I was fooling myself even being there. But I was still a kid, and there was something so romantic and exciting being around those wonderful planes. To this day, though my wife hates it, I still jump at the chance to fly with my friends whenever possible.

11. Hey Lance— I mean Mr. Armstrong. Please move over and let me pass!

I know what follows will be interesting for you, because it's not only fact but a facet of a man's life that was not only a metamorphosis but a final burial of a large slice of freedom. I'm talking about a love affair with wheels. Before you roll your eyes and picture a skinny kid riding up and down the street with playing cards attached by clothes pins to his bike's spokes, read on, because I promise you'll be entertained. As you shake your head, amazed at what an unbelievable jackass I was for doing the things I attempted, remember something I wrote earlier: those with poor vision don't realize what it's like to have normal sight. They don't know what they're not seeing!

Around age fourteen or so, every low-vision boy in America begins thinking about the same things every other teen-ager has on his mind: chicks, music, sports, and of course—cars. One of the most difficult things in the world to deal with when you have poor vision is the realization that you're not going to be able to drive. Everyone can tell you it's not important; it doesn't make you less of a person or man; it's no big thing to chicks that you can't drive; there are millions of people in the world who don't drive, etc., etc. They can say what they want, but in the U.S., driving is a rite of passage for teen boys, particularly in California.

To this day, I love cars, especially sports models, and have owned (but only dreamed of driving) some beautiful automobiles. I listen to the Indy 500 every year, keep a casual knowledge of Formula 1 and NASCAR racing, and try to stay on top of new automobile technology. I know a good reason for my interest in cars was Floyd's hobby of racing hard-tops, midget racers, and a few flirting moments with drag racing after he got the family back on our

43

feet after the great flood. But here's the truth, from the time I was ten, I never liked getting my hands greasy, never did well helping Floyd under the chassis or hood because of my lack of night vision and absence of usable sight in dark places. Believe me, using the hunt, touch, and cuss method while working on a car engine is not a really wise move! He taught me to drive a stick shift before I was twelve but knew full well, I wasn't seeing what I should. But like so many people raising children with disabilities, he had a difficult time dealing with reality. In his way, he wanted me to be like the other boys.

Things had disintegrated a lot at home and helping Floyd with his cars was one of the few things we could share. During high school, even before I was old enough to get a permit, he bought me a car. I know he had convinced himself I would somehow get a license, for the eye tests were far less comprehensive at that time. It was a little white Triumph TR3, a small four-cylinder convertible sports car with twin SU carburetors, wire wheels and a four-speed floor-mounted stick transmission. Floyd would take me out to the Pleasanton Valley and let me drive around the nearly deserted roads. Of course, I absolutely loved the experience and naturally we were both fooling ourselves into believing I could get a license.

On one weekday after school when the folks were out of town for some reason, I took the keys to the TR3 and decided to take a ride around the neighborhood where there was little traffic and even less police presence for that matter. I stopped a few blocks down the way and picked up Sandy, a fun-loving fellow student I'd been dating. She knew I didn't have a license, but it didn't bother her in the least. An hour later, after stopping at the local A and W root beer and burger joint, I dropped her off safely a few houses down from her house, hoping her parents didn't see who was driving the car. I turned down our home street, still filled with the euphoria of having a sweet time with Sandy and getting away with something but not causing any harm. Trying to concentrate on the road ahead, I glanced in the small rear-view mirror mounted on the windshield of the little British gem. Instantly the wind was driven from my lungs as if I'd been punched in the plexus by Mike Tyson. Directly behind me, a tiny child, no more than three years old, was riding a tricycle near the middle of the street. He must have darted out from in between two parked cars, for I hadn't seen him at all. I know I couldn't have missed the little guy by more than a few inches! I was shaking violently and near vomiting as I pulled up in front of the house, and after that episode of stupidity, for over a decade, I refused to touch a set of car keys (even just to open the trunk).

Of course, I had been riding a bicycle for years delivering *The Daily Review* (the local print bugle). Here's a small side bar:

The newspaper group eventually supplied me with more stuff than any Walmart store. I would go out nights with the circulation managers and sell subscriptions door to door. I suppose I was given a gift, for I soon had set many records selling the paper to new folks moving into the area. One evening in Livermore, when the paper opened up delivery to that new and growing area, I sold seventy-four new accounts. At first, I was given prizes for my efforts: sports and stereo equipment, skateboards, powered model airplanes, etc., but soon I began competing in some large sales contests. I won five trips to Disneyland, one trip to Catalina, and the one I'm most proud of: a two-week vacation for Anne and me to Waikiki Beach in Hawaii. By my second year of high school, I had stopped delivering papers and was working full time on commission as a subscription canvasser. Floyd was tough and made me buy all my own school clothes and personal items, and I thank him for that to this day. It taught me to respect money, be independent, and budget funds. Now back to the wheels.

Those with normal vision would have a difficult time understanding the deep longing and anger a teenager with a disability keeps inside when they find they won't be able to do all the same activities their friends take for granted—like getting a driver's license. When I was forced to face this truth head on, I tried to find the most viable substitute for having a car, so I turned to my old companion the bicycle. I bought a used American ten-speed racing bike and used it daily to get around town. Of course, I knew my vision was very poor, but I had learned a very complicated and unique method of scanning the road ahead, and clearing over my shoulder before making turns, especially in traffic. The term for this technique of using usable vision is: "eccentric viewing" (And please remember, at that time I had no idea I was going blind).

Even though I was taking a monumental chance of someday having a crash, the exhilaration of riding was not only intoxicating but physically challenging. I was never able to ride at night, but daylight cycling gave me independence and the feeling of not being impaired or stifled of freedom. I despised being tied to having to rely on someone else every time I wanted to go somewhere. I began hanging around the cycling shops, and the bike became my friend and greatest tool.

My senior year, six months before the U.S. Army engulfed my mortal soul, I became the owner of my most prized purchase to that point of my life. Overnight I was the proudest non-car driver in Northern California. I took delivery of the Ferrari of racing bicycles: a Cinelli Super Corsa LTD road racer (the c's are pronounced as "ch") built in Cino Cinelli's shop in Milan, Italy to my pre-measured leg length and height.

The deposit for the order was almost an adult's month's wages, and I had to wait almost six months for it to be delivered. I learned later it was one of the first fifteen speed racing bikes in the Bay Area. It had all Campagnolo parts and accessories (at that time the best available), and center-pull cabled brakes with road racing wheel rims utilizing the fragile sew-up high pressure tires (the dream and nightmare of all serious road riders). Built for professional racers (Cino had been a champion rider himself), the machine was constructed from custom alloys and Cino's new invention: aluminum alloy racing handlebars with cushioned tape. Though it had a steel frame, certainly heavier than the carbon-fiber frames of today, with another Cinelli innovation: the plastic lined, calf-skin saddle, it was one of the lightest road cycles in the world. Believe me, it rode like the wind.

For nearly three years, I rode the back roads of Northern California, many thousands of miles, and my Italian beauty was a source of conversation everywhere I rode it. Naturally, I couldn't leave it unguarded for any length of time, and even with the most advanced locks of the time, I never left it in public areas for more than ten minutes.

To tell some exciting episodes of riding right here would confuse the chronology of the book, so as you read on, I'll share some very hairy and wild adventures I experienced while riding my Milanese pride and joy. Cino Cinelli's black masterpiece met a fatal end, but I lived to walk another day!

12. The Army Goes Rolling Along

The summer after graduating from high school, some of my closest friends decided to join the U.S. Army. I'd already taken my college entrance qualification tests, and my folks expected me to begin in the fall. After hours of pleading, Floyd talked Anne into letting me go with the guys to the Oakland Army Terminal for the induction program. I was legally blind, so my friends thought I was insane. I explained to them I didn't want to be left behind, but none of them believed I would get past the front door.

We spent the morning filling out forms, answering questions, and taking preliminary tests. From my junior year in high school, I had learned to use a small handheld circular magnifier and could hide it very well in my hand. I had no birth certificate, so I was able to use my baptismal record from the church for a substitute (the reason for not having a birth certificate is part of the rest of the mystery later revealed to me).

I passed the general physical with ease, but of course, my greatest fear was the upcoming eye test. When we broke for lunch, with a glimmer of hope, I made my way to the vision center I'd passed earlier that morning and was excited to find no one in the room. In minutes, I'd memorized the first eight lines of the eye chart, forming the letters into nonsense words. Two days later, I was a member of the U.S. Army. During the light of day, I'd become a master of faking I could see, for I had usable vision in both eyes. But I had no interest in guns, tanks, bombs, or anything remotely capable of making a loud noise or causing me permanent bodily harm. My only interests were communications, codes, and ciphering.

The following week we were bused to the training center at Fort Ord, California. The next four months were a true odyssey. The daily routine is now a total blur, but I did my best at everything the army threw at me. I soon found little indignation when called a slime-sucking pig, choosing to believe that in truth, I was mentally far better equipped to accept the challenges of slime sucking then any of my degenerate drill instructors. I was a model soldier, keeping my mouth shut and my ears open. Not having any night vision (except for bright lights), every day I hoped the brass wouldn't discover I couldn't see. I remember running in full battle gear across the sand dunes of the night infiltration course near the beaches of the Pacific Ocean. Dozens of times, I fell in or over some ditch or stretch of wire. My buddy Del would yell "up" if it was high, or "over" if I needed to jump. Fortunately, I was in the best shape of my life, because that night my body took more punishment than a terrorist at an NRA convention!

There is a fine program in Albany, California: The Orientation Center for the Blind (OCB). At this site, young adults are taught the techniques necessary for mobility and travel in public. Some of the students jokingly refer to the program as "Ouch. Crash. Bang." After that night on the beach in Monterey, I'll always feel like an honorary member.

With a little heavenly guidance or maybe a great deal of luck, I somehow made it through boot camp. I passed the initial testing for Counter Measures Intelligence School in Fort Devins, Massachusetts, and was marking time at the Fort Ord base to be shipped out east. One afternoon, I was walking past one of the softball fields, when a group of troops started yelling at me to come and play, since they were short a player on one side. I said I wasn't interested, but their chiding and taunts (and the sudden appearance at my side of Nikko, a six-three Greco Roman wrestler from our neighboring platoon) soon found me on the field. It was one of those bright days when, with a fatigue cap to cut the glare from the corner of my left or "good" eye, I could see the flight of the large softball (unlike the smaller, faster hard ball) part of the time. I talked my way into playing right field, for the majority of the troops were hitting to left. But a big left-handed African American kid from another battalion came to bat. On the second pitch he crushed the ball high in the air, and I thought I saw it leave the bat in my direction. I turned and started running, knowing from the sound of the bat he'd hit it a ton.

To this day I swear I thought I saw the ball coming down close enough for me to catch it (it was probably a damned seagull!), but as I was running full speed my soon to be miraculous catch was rudely interrupted by a monumental collision. The Russian judge gave me a perfect ten, however the French judge said my form needed improvement and was critical of my music selection, giving me a rude 9.3. I ran full speed into a wooden piling-and-plank exercise demonstration platform, at least eight feet high and ten feet in diameter! I "came to" a few minutes later and was carried to the infirmary. It took some stitches to close some gashes on my head, and I nearly ripped off the lobe of my left ear, but thankfully had no broken bones. I soon was the proud owner of two magnificent black eyes and a pair of shattered glasses.

Three days later, though I could still barely walk, the Platoon Sergeant forced me to go to the eye clinic to get new lenses. I knew the game was up. The clinic was packed with recruits, and the corpsman was swamped. Suddenly the door opened, and an officer walked in, looking as if he'd just stepped out of the Pentagon. His blouse was laden with decorations and bars, and as he came near, I could make out the scrambled eggs on his officer's cap. He was a Lt. Colonel from Walter Reed Hospital on his way through Ord on an inspection tour.

"Let me give you a hand, soldier," he said to the corpsman as he removed his coat. I slid even lower on my chair, while one word echoed in my head: "Busted!" Only minutes later, as the Lt. Colonel looked into my eyes with that blasted light I'd seen at least a hundred times before, he cursed loudly, "Sweet Jesus Christ, son, how in hell did you ever get in the Army of the United States? In thirty years, I've never seen retinas this bad." His words ended my illustrious military career. I spent the next month in Letterman Hospital at the Presidio of San Francisco, undergoing endless tests and procedures, waiting for an unwanted medical discharge. In only a few short days, I'd had my fill of medical personnel passing through or just curious, waking me up in the middle of the night to look in my eyes. At that time there were only two diagnosed cases of Retinitis Pigmentosa in the Sixth Army, and I was one of them. I filled my time at Letterman entertaining the patients in the wards, playing music and joking with the ones who felt good enough to laugh, and teaching some of the injured troops to play guitar and sing. Even then, I guess, I was thinking like a teacher, trying to find ways to help guys learn to play. I was proud for I became friends with a fellow from North Carolina who had lost his right arm in a mortar misfire. He had a warm baritone voice and loved country music and had played drums in an amateur band before going into the service.

I had heard of the Wagner touch system of playing the electric guitar and did a little research. We got hold of a used, inexpensive solid-body electric guitar and small amp. I lowered the strings on the guitar as low as possible and replaced the heavy strings with the lightest I could find at the time. Then, I tuned the guitar to an open chord tuning. This means if you strum across the strings without placing any fingers on the fretboard it sounds a major chord. Many slide lap guitars played with a steel bar slid up and down the neck is tuned in this manner. I taught him to squeeze the neck, laying his left index finger across all six strings ("barring," in modern terms) and then sliding up to the fifth fret and then using the ring and pinky fingers of the same hand, he could strum across the strings, sliding from open to fifth and seventh frets to get the three major chords. With these three chords, anyone could sing ten thousand songs. By the time I left, only less than a month later, he sounded fantastic!

My last memory of the U.S. Army was walking down a sidewalk in San Francisco headed for the Transbay Bus Terminal. With my honorable discharge in my pocket, I felt so lonesome and dejected there were tears in my eyes. To add to my despair, as I passed a rowdy beer joint, echoing from inside, came the driving beat of the late Ray Charles song: "Hit the Road Jack" (and don't ya come back no more). An old saying from the south came to mind: "Brother, I can't get no lower, the dirt's in the way." At the time, I had no way of knowing my divorce from Uncle Sam would be an unreturnable gift, for only a month later, I registered late and entered college.

13. Hail to the Spartans!

I began classes at San Jose State University that fall semester and immediately fell into the scholarly scene, finding very soon that I loved it. My trumpet teacher heard me sing and promptly took the horn away from me. He took me down the hall to one of the voice teachers and that was the end of my threat to Miles Davis. In only a few months, I had joined the Opera Workshop. What a blast! Meet buxom women and getting to wear tights! Like all the neophytes must, I began singing in the chorus. One of my earliest screw-ups was in a production of "La Perichole," a comic opera by Jacques Offenbach (one of those German composers who spent most of his life in France, loving Pâté and champagne more than bratwurst and beer). During one scene in the opera, a nobleman was to ride into town on a live donkey. The role of the Viceroy, dressed in flowing robes and a tall Pope-like headpiece, was sung by a tall young man. His feet nearly touched the floor as he rode the animal on stage. My buddy Simpson, standing next to me center stage near a fake staircase, had only one line to deliver: "Hail, the Viceroy!" We were dressed as palace guards, complete with sandals, swords, and helmets. Simpson carried a tall, spear-like scepter with a wooden disc on top. We immediately dubbed it his "radioactive pizza cutter."

On opening night, as the scene unfolded, the chorus bellowed as the Monarch entered. As the donkey approached center stage near the palace steps, Simpson raised his staff to slam it onto the step twice and then deliver his only line in the opera, "Hail the Viceroy". I didn't see the base of the pole in the dim light, and as I stepped to the side, I inadvertently bumped the shaft with my arm as it came down on the second step of the fake stairs. The bottom of the pole missed the stairs, and to the shock of everyone, swung forward hitting the unsuspecting Viceroy (now facing the audience) square on the head, knocking off his Papal headpiece. As the donkey bowed down and backed up in fright, the de-donkeyed Viceroy was left standing on the stage as the now frightened animal pulled loose from the two cast members leading it. It galloped across the stage, disappearing into the darkness. The audience roared. The cast fell apart, but soon picked up the pieces, and the show forged on. The tall and beautiful lyric soprano lead, one of my first secret heartthrobs in the music world, was magnificent and soon stole the show. Mr. Simpson, his weapon removed, was relegated to a lesser station in the Viceroy's court for the final performances.

Only a few months later, I asked the soprano (just mentioned) for a date to see the stage production of West Side Story in San Francisco and to have dinner at Fisherman's Wharf. She owned a Porsche sports car, and I was blown away when she said yes. What followed was the wildest, most unlikely week of my life to that point.

Margot was born in Munich, Germany, and her family was very wealthy. They owned a large import liquor and wine distribution corporation on the East Coast. She was eight years older, was six-foot tall, over an inch taller than me, and I never asked her why she was going to SJSU instead of CAL or one of the local private colleges. It was Christmas break, and I had nowhere to go. Floyd, my stepdad, and I weren't talking, and there's nothing worse than being alone on the holidays. I guess Margot felt the same, for those four days we spent together were filled with passion, warmth, and flat out "lust"— something out of a movie.

Margot shared a beautiful apartment near Alum Rock Park in San Jose and her roommate, an x-ray tech at the local hospital had gone back East to spend the holidays with family. I had been around the block a few times in the past few years and was told I wasn't too hard to look at, but I would be a liar if I said I didn't still have very vivid memories of that Christmas Eve. I remember her telling me as we lay on the rug near the Small Christmas tree in front of the fireplace, that when she made love again, it would be to the music of Beethoven. Even today, next to Mozart, he's my favorite classical composer

The summer of that new year, Margot decided to go to Paris to study voice and had a chance to sing in the French subsidized operas. I spent a solid month moaning my loss and trying to crawl up out of the abyss of "lost love."

Gradually as my nasal tenor opened and filled out, I began to audition for singing solo roles. The beginning of my sophomore year, I won the part of Alfred, Rosalinda's lover in another bit of foolishness, "Die Fledermaus." One can imagine my surprise, when at the first rehearsal, I found my lyric lover was five months pregnant! She had a great sense of humor and we soon managed to get over the musical "hump."

From the start, my role was a disaster, both from nerves and inexperience and a tyrannical director. He once told me I possessed the stage presence of a drunken plumber. I was honored, deciding this was a monumental advancement from a slime-sucking pig. During the first performance, I stumbled on stage after my lover's husband had been hauled off to jail and tried to blurt out my big line, "Rosalinda, finally my love. He's in jail, and we're alone." Laughter rolled through the audience as I bellowed, "Rosalinda, my love. Finally, we're in jail, and he's alone!"

In another scene I was supposed to be standing in the courtyard, singing up to Rosalinda in her chambers. She spoke to her maid, "Oh, there's my lover, Alfred. He's here again to serenade me with his high C." At that moment, I was supposed to sing a sustained high note in answer to her words. I've been fortunate, and still am, to have a "C" in my voice, but I didn't have a pitch pipe, and the note I selected was somewhere near the shriek of an alley cat or ambulance siren. The sound that issued forth from my trembling mouth will never be forgotten in San Jose State opera annals. A local newspaper reviewer remarked the following day, "The note 'sung' from the courtyard by the young tenor singing the role of Alfred was...was...unbelievable!"

Thankfully my voice continued to grow as fast as my confidence. But my eyesight kept me in a constant state of "pinch-drawers" (as my Drill Sergeant used to say). Once after finishing one of my favorite arias, "Il Mio Tesoro," from Mozart's *Don Giovanni*, I rushed off stage right as the curtain closed. My exit was flawless except for one small detail. Earlier, someone had left a large, hand-held metal and glass lantern on the floor offstage. I kicked it solidly enough to have annihilated Tom Dempsey's current NFL field goal record. This record was assured if the stage wall hadn't stopped the flight of the shattered lantern ten feet in the air! I know it took an hour to sweep up the broken glass.

At the end of the next semester, we performed another comic opera by Mozart, *Cosi Fan Tutti*. At one point in the farcical plot, I came on stage to sing, "Una Aura Amorosa," a beautiful lyrical aria of love. As I made my way slowly on stage, one of the ladies near me accidently dropped a small artificial bouquet she was holding, and it landed on my right foot. Of course, being the consummate gentleman, I am, I bent over to graciously pick it up as if the act was part of the scene.

The thin breeches of my Baroque costume were skintight, and I wore an athletic jock strap because men's underwear showed through the material. As I bent deeply and grasped the posies, the entire rear end of my pants exploded with a thundering rip (something approaching a resounding elephant fart!), and the lightning speed the vagrant bouquet was delivered would be envied by any FTD florist in the country. My beautiful aria was delivered to the audience with my legs together and my back straight, making me look much like a seventeenth century mannikin or a member of the Black Watch Guard. As various giggles and snorts issued behind me on stage, in my air-conditioned state, I then exited the scene backward. I tried to acknowledge the audience's applause, but there was no way in Mozart I was going to bow!

14. Where's the fire buddy? In your eyes officer, in your eyes!

I kept my Cinelli locked up in the boarding house and rode it to college every day. One morning, I had overslept and was really hauling rear down the streets to make my first class. I had already worn out my welcome with the professor because of chronic tardiness and frequent naps (part of the semester, I had been working graveyard at the United Can Plant). I flew past an elementary school, weaving between slow moving cars and parked vehicles on the right. I was nearly at the campus, passing in front of the men's dormitories, when I nearly jumped off the saddle of my Corsa. My ears were greeted with a short wail of a police siren. I glanced back over my left shoulder and couldn't believe what I saw. Behind me was a city police car. I pulled over to the right, slowing down, expecting him to pass me as I thought he needed to do. As he pulled next to me, a laconic voice on a speaker told me to pull off the street and stop.

My hart began to pound as I jumped off my bike, and then I heard a few catcalls coming from the three-story dorms behind me. As the officer pulled over and got out of the squad car, a few more taunts were launched from the windows of the dorms: "Hey blue boy, who did he murder?"

As he walked up to me, out of habit I removed the riding helmet from my head and waited for him to speak. "Looks like you're in a big hurry this morning, correct?" He was young, not more than six or so years older than me. "Hey pig, can't you find anything better to do with the taxpayer's money?" I felt my stature shrink as the taunts increased.

"Yes sir," I answered, still not knowing what was coming, "I'm late for a Geology class, and we're taking an exam today."

"Sorry buddy, but that or any excuse, isn't going to help you. You were going nearly ten miles over the speed limit back there at the school and doing a lot of weaving between cars."

"Hey badge-man, how long you been in the cookie jar commandoes?" I remember thinking: "You guys are frying me, for God's sake, put a sock in it!" I didn't have to have 20-20 to see the color rising in the young officer's face as he checked out my ID. He seemed exasperated I didn't have a driver's license. "Better check his shorts for concealed drugs and weapons. He looks dangerous!" This time the officer looked back at the dude yelling from the second-floor window. He turned back and began writing savagely on a tablet of blank citations he carried, and I knew I'd had it.

"I promise sir; from now on I'll be really careful and won't ride so fast in traffic."

My plea was ignored as he answered, "You should have thought of that course some time ago, the law is the law, and it's there for the safety of all of us. I'd suggest you take care of this immediately."

"Police brutality! Overuse of authority and force!" rang from another of the dorm's students, who were now really getting into the game. His coloring was even deeper as he ripped the ticket off the book and thrust it in my direction. "Slap on the cuffs and club his ass. He's on his way to get his mommy a quart of milk!" I quickly folded the ticket and shoved it into my Inside breaker pocket, silently hoping he'd leave quickly before, with the assistance of my dorm cheer leaders, I found myself in San Quentin for some obscure infraction. "Check that damned seat-bag, oinker! He's carrying a grenade in there!"

I mumbled a silent "thank you" as he roared off down the street, knowing I'd been fortunate to get a ticket only for speeding, and had not received an additional fine for reckless driving.

"Hey man, go on and get that milk, and get yourself a bottle of Jack Daniels while you're at it." I ignored the quip; the officer had only been doing his job and I knew damn well I had been major league stupid that morning. I didn't fight the ticket, but when I paid the fine, the clerk said it was the first time in nearly twenty years of working traffic court, he'd seen a moving violation for speeding on a bicycle. Remember, as I said earlier, my Cinelli rode like the wind!

15. Can I Get Your Attention Please!

On a daily basis, I was learning to accept and deal with my gradually diminishing remaining vision, but I can't adequately remember the size of the chip on my shoulder. In retrospect, I'm ashamed to admit it may have been slightly larger than life itself. I'd met a particularly healthy and straight-out gorgeous lady, Lorraine. Like Margot, she later broke my sensitive heart, but that's another edge to my "weapon of success. One evening, I'd arranged to meet her on the third floor of the new library building on the corner of the old campus. I'd planned to take her out for pizza, and perhaps some extensive "rehearsing" later in the evening. Upon entering the library reading room, I was greeted by a sour-faced woman in her thirties, who I'm sure would have much rather been at home, eating pizza, and "rehearsing." My guitar case banged into a file cabinet next to her desk, and I was told tersely to, "keep it down."

I walked through the bar of the "moo" stall and started looking for Lorraine. After searching one side of the room, I walked back to the other side of the aisle. Hurrying, I didn't see the metal trashcan sitting near the end of a table. My errant guitar case struck the empty can, knocking it over, rolling it down the aisle. The metallic clatter was amplified in the sterility of the tiled room.

Of course, the top of the can was a larger diameter than the bottom, so as it rolled it made a slow turn to the left. As though guided by a computer on a deep space probe, it made a neat turn under the gate of the "moo" stall and rolled down the stairwell I'd just walked up minutes before.

I gritted my teeth, waiting for at least a week for the can to stop bouncing down the stairs and come to a merciful rest on the landing below. I knew then and forever the meaning of the term "deafening silence." I knew every eye in the room was staring at me, so I said the only thing that entered my numbed mind, "Well folks, now that I have your attention, is lovely Lorraine ready to leave?" At the time, she was ready to amputate my guitar case and my head, but we laughed about that night for months.

16. What a Gas!

Using some of the extravagant riches I'd amassed while working for Uncle Sam, I was able to get a room fairly near the campus at a local boarding house. Mrs. Kelly, the owner of the less-than-majestic building, was a close facsimile to my earlier babysitter of "exploding peaches" fame. Shall we say, she would have loved being employed by Guinness Breweries as a quality control supervisor. Most of the boarders found her to be too crotchety, but luckily, because of my knowledge of some aging Celtic folksongs, the small Irish lady took a liking to me, and on the weekends when meals weren't provided, allowed me to cook in her kitchen for some of the guys and myself. Had they known my questionable culinary past and "dumpling" expertise, I'm sure they would never have elevated me to weekend chef; but quite frankly, none of the guys knew enough about stoves to warm a stale pizza.

For the first month or so I turned out one smashing success after another: luscious casseroles made from macaroni, cubed Spam, mushroom soup, and cheese whiz; meat loaf; garlic pork chops and fried potatoes with onions; and even a chewy chocolate sheet cake with white butter cream frosting. But the shipwreck causing my ultimate demise and dethroning in the kitchen was an honest mistake. Baking was not at the top of my kitchen skills, but I had a cursory knowledge of a few recipes. I had often in past years helped Anne make homemade bread and rolls and enjoyed playing with the dough. I'm sure in the act of "dough manipulation," there's some goofy Freudian tie-in with frustrated sexual inadequacies or superiorities, or maybe just "Hey, this is like playing in the mud when I was a kid."

I beat feet down to the small Chinese grocery on the corner and picked up the ingredients for making four loaves of bread. The only snag was that Mr. Leong, the elf-like grocer, didn't have any of the flat packages of dry yeast like Anne always used. All he had were some large squares of Fleischmann's wet yeast. With my magnificent flare for improvisation, I figured it would be a fine substitute.

Back in the kitchen that Saturday afternoon, I cranked up the Giants game on my transistor radio, and "Ready! Set! Cook!" With only a couple of tablespoons of olive oil in the dough, it turned out silky and fragrant. Most of the fragrance was coming from the huge amount of yeast I'd used in the mixture. I greased the baking loaf pans, and a couple of hours later, after letting the dough rise, pre-set the oven and pushed the dough down in the pans for the final rise before baking. I should have known from the speed of the dough rising the second time something was drastically amiss, but it sure smelled fabulous. By now, some of the guys around the house were sticking their noses in the kitchen to see what I was up to. The news got around fast I was making fresh bread. In the other side of Mrs. Kelly's big double ovens, I placed the other pan of tuna noodle casserole I'd made the night before, and after piercing their casings with a fork, placed a large package of Italian sausages in a skillet. I heard somewhere that untold numbers of neophyte chefs have been seriously maimed or permanently emasculated by exploding Polish, German, or Italian sausages. Because of their pork content, they are presently being explored in a well-known Middle Eastern country as weapons of mass destruction.

In only a half-hour, the aroma of the baking bread permeated the boarding house and wafted throughout the neighborhood. When I opened the oven to check on my masterpieces, I was amazed at the height and beauty of the browning crowns of each loaf. Perhaps due to the pleadings from some of the boarders, I soon made my second unforced error. The loaves looked so good, I failed to leave them in the oven long enough to finish baking to the centers. The loaves never made it to the dinner table. Wiping out nearly a pound of butter, the crew demolished my still warm bread with the ferocity of Nero Wolfe. Of course, there was one small problem, which in an hour or so, became a much larger and more fragrant issue. The bread had not reached a high enough temperature in the center to kill the activity of the wet yeast and it was now working its own particular magic in the innards of my unsuspecting roommates!

The old building was soon a candidate for seismic retrofitting from the concussive assaults on its walls and supporting structures. The ensuing gaseous outbursts for the next twelve hours would have easily filled both the Goodyear and Fuji blimps. Finding matches and room deodorizer became a bartering item of high demand. After a few hours, I decided in order to live to bake another day, it was in my best interest to sneak out the back and go visit lovely Lorraine. Thank God I had the good sense to never bake bread for her. Hey, now that I think of it, maybe she found out about my evil deed, and that's why a year later, she dumped me for the ski instructor with the Austin-Healy. Here baby— have a piece of this warm bread!

17. Right Place, Right Time

You'd think my run-in with the exercise platform in the Army and my rude treatment by the French judge would be enough to keep me out of any semblance of athletic endeavors forever, but alas, I still believed somewhere there was one last moment of glory left for me. From about age twelve, I have always loved the game of basketball. During those early years, I could still see well enough to watch and play. There's always been something poetic and graceful about the act of shooting and rebounding, and acrobatic moves in the air. Obviously with my eyesight, I didn't have much of a chance, but despite the many times I blew it big time, I kept trying to play.

I had one uncanny ability that stayed with me even after I lost almost all my vision. I could shoot free-throws at over eighty percent and could handle the ball well. I loved to drive the lane, cut off pick and rolls, and could shoot with either hand (of course where the ball came down was another matter!). It's almost impossible to explain how I did it. Even into my twenties, when I drove the lane and got close enough to the backboard, I could see the bracket assembly where the hoop is bolted to the backboard and sometimes even the square border painted above the hoop. That's all I needed. My biggest problem was trying to rebound or take fast passes from any of my teammates. Of course, that's two thirds of the game! I must have taken a basketball off the head or privates so many times my face should look like the ghost of the star of *Rocky XII*, and it's no wonder my voice has remained so high!

I hated playing full court and especially with five men on a side (amazing, isn't that two thirds of the game?). My favorite situation was one on one, but I could play a limited game of hunch or three men on a side, half court. Folks, I'm not going to lay a romanticized tale of what a great round ball player I was, because the Pope would look more at home on the court than I did; but I spent hours trying to play because I loved the game so much. It was a sickness.

My fraternity Phi Mu Alpha got a team together to play in the intramurals and I promptly became our greatest rooter and bench warmer. We only had seven players when they all showed up, but for a bunch of flaky musicians, we weren't too bad (All right, we were awful, there I go romanticizing again!). We hadn't won a game in six tries and were well on our way to not winning another when our best guard, a little tuba player named Eddie, got in a scuffle with an opposing player and was asked by the ref to take an immediate scenic tour of the locker room. Sitting with my heart banging in my chest, I prayed Mike, our willowy reserve swingman would make it through the rest of the game. Mike won the task of guarding a very talented and big-mouthed young man from Oakland Tech who'd been quite a star in high school. Every time this trash-talker would take a shot, he'd yell, "Well baby, here it is!" The maddening thing was, that the majority of the time the damn ball would land in the bucket. We were losing by nearly thirty points, and everyone in the gym, including some of the sparse spectators, were getting sick of hearing those shouted words. With only four minutes left in the game, Jim, our six-four Latvian-Swedish center and the only guy on the team that could really play, rolled his ankle and had to be helped off the court. One of our forwards (I don't remember his name), moved over to center and yours truly had to take the court.

My God, you'd think I had just been inserted in the NBA All-Star Game. I was shaking so bad my teeth were chattering. Now, let's crank this pup up a few more notches!! To my horror, I heard from behind me the unmistakable alto of Lorraine, my true love, saying something like, "Go get em' Tiger! Or maybe it was "Go get 'em Pope." I just don't remember. I was too scared. I told the guys not to throw me the ball unless they yelled my name and not to pass it to me on cuts to the basket. Maybe my movement would open a path to the bucket for them- Hey, isn't that a moving screen?

Playing the right guard position, I had the court on my left side where I could follow some of the action out of the corner of my left eye and didn't have to worry too much about my right side because of the sideline of the court. My first trip down court on defense, I found myself trying to identify a pair of hairy kneecaps as "our friend" who took a rising jump shot and announced, "Well, there it is." I didn't need to turn my head to try and see if the shot went in. I heard the clean swish and snap of the ball falling through the net. It seemed this same routine was repeated at least three times in the next few minutes. When we were back on offense, Mike cut behind me and I rolled to the right toward the baseline. I heard Roy and turned in time to grab and fumble a short bounce pass into my chest. I spun and in the same motion, fired an eighteen-foot jumper that banked off the backboard and went in the bucket. Of course, I had no intention of shooting it off the backboard. It was a prayer. That was the only points I ever scored in a real organized game in college.

While sitting on the bench earlier, I noticed "our friend" had one move he'd mastered, and it was consistent. He loved to drive the left baseline and go across the lane, laying the ball up from the right side of the hoop (called a cross under lay-up). He'd back-doored Jim, our center, on the move twice in the first half of the game. With only a minute left in the debacle, he made another of his patented jump shots making his usual announcement and started back down court. Just over half-court, one of their players stole the ball from Mike and we turned, running back on defense. It was beautiful, as if in a play book. They went into their usual set offense, and I saw "our friend" cutting across the court from the left baseline as I ran flat out down the side of the key on the right. As their big forward set a vicious pick on our reserve center, I knew what was coming so I didn't try to get into "our friend's" path to the basket, but rather cut across the top of the right side of the key jumping as high as I could, aiming for an imaginary spot on the right side of the basket. I'd always been a good jumper and have a scar half the length of my ring finger on my right hand from showing off after a lay-up, grabbing the rim, getting the finger caught on a sharp piece of metal on an outside bucket, the "mouth." I closed in in only a second, and to my utter amazement, I made a clean opened handed block on his lay-up, knocking it fifteen feet into the racks of folding chairs against the wall at the end of the court. A bunch of the chairs slid down, clattering and making a great bunch of racket from the hardwood floor. It was total luck! Acting as cool as I possibly could while floating five feet off the floor, I quickly spun away and hustled back down court to my position. But there, at that moment, I experienced an exhilarating high I will never forget. I bellowed as loud as I could, "Well baby- there it is!!"

18. Two Pounds in a One Pound Can

Whenever I could, I'd pack my small rear pack on my Cinelli and take off for the beach roads or the Central Valley. Often, it was with friends and other avid cyclists, but many times, I went alone. It was important to study the maps that were available at cycle shops. For this task, my little magnifier was invaluable. One of the most maddening occurrences maddening occurrences (if you didn't do your homework) was to ride for miles and then have to retrace your route because of a bottleneck where bikers could not traverse or were forbidden to do so. Dozens of times, I swallowed my cyclist's pride and hitched rides in the rear of pickups rather than retrace an eight-mile route to get around a freeway bottleneck. The two most thrilling rides I remember were my trips to Yosemite Valley and the little town of Groveland near Pine Mountain Lake at the top of Old Priest Grade. This was one of the steepest climbs I ever saw. Cycling is like so many other sporting events, it's a lot more fun coming down the slope than going up. I don't have the words to describe the *high* experienced coming down a twisting mountain road on a racing bicycle. Of course, with my poor vision, it was inevitable I would crash. The interesting thing is, the two worst crashes I experienced were not due to my eyesight.

My first brain-ringing wake-up call was very near where I had lived and gone to high school. Tucked behind the Hayward Hills in the East Bay area is a lovely section of land named Palomares Canyon. It connects the Dublin Canyon near Castro Valley to the Niles Canyon cutting back over the Hayward fault to the city of Fremont, just north of the Old Mission San Jose. I had ridden this route dozens of times over the years and knew nearly every turn of the snaking, paved road. From the Castro Valley side of the canyon, the ride climbs gradually for many miles, then becomes steeper, then drops off and descends at a much more severe grade as the road snakes down to the Old Niles Canyon road. Niles Canyon ends near the historic railroad town of Niles (in the early 1900's, many silent pictures were filmed there.

The last time I rode the canyon was very early on a cold and windless morning. I had reached the peak of the grade and had begun the steep descent on the southern slope. About halfway down the grade, I had gained a great deal of speed, but my Corsa's rigid frame held the line so well, my balance on the turns was exquisite. I heard an engine behind me, and as I glanced back, I caught sight of a dark colored pickup. There were many ranches and estates along the canyon and many of the vehicles on the road were trucks with an occasional commuter car cutting through to avoid the early-morning traffic.

This person pulled up right on my tail and wouldn't get off. I was riding on the canyon side of the road and had no place to pull off to let him pass, and the road at that time was too narrow to just stop. Another minute went by and then the guy leaned on his horn, wanting me to get out of his way. I braked as slowly as I could, trying not to overheat my rims and roll a tire on a turn, looking for a pull-off at one of the turns. I remember being frustrated that I didn't recall where one was located. I guess my slowing down pissed the guy off even more, for on the approach to the next right turn of the canyon, he pulled up next to me. I could have reached out and touched his right front fender. Had I known what was about to occur, I would have spat on it.

Suddenly, as I braked with my entire grip, I realized what was about to happen. He cut the angle of the turn, and as I think back on the crash, I don't think he had a choice. He would have hit the mountain on his left at the speed he was traveling. Quite simply, I ran out of road— there wasn't enough space for both of us. The next thing I remember was crashing through brush and branches, staying on the bike for a few bounces and then being airborne. I can thank Mother Nature for not having serious injuries, for the young trees and shrubs on the down slope of the canyon had broken my fall. My bike hung up on the brush above and behind me, while I came to rest another twenty feet down the side near a small creek. The fall knocked the breath out of me, and as I finally began to move, the only severe pain I felt was in my neck. I knew I wasn't paralyzed because I could move all my extremities, but later I found I had jammed my neck badly; it continued to give me an occasional stiff neck for years to come. Except for some deep scrapes and scratches, I was okay. By a miracle, my Corsa was not badly damaged either, and with a few adjustments, I had it back on the canyon road in about twenty minutes. The puke that ran me off the road never stopped to see if I was injured. I'm bitter to this day. People often don't realize cyclists need space too, that they can't just evaporate from your path when you want them too.

In a strange twist, I was very blessed, for the next severe right turn down the canyon had a nearly straight-down drop of nearly seventy feet. If the crash had happened at this drop, I would've been a dead duck. How many lives is a cat allowed to use?

19. Oops! Colorblind!

Back at SJSU, I continued my voice lessons and was fortunate to be taken as a student by the magnificent tenor and teacher, Fredrick Lorwicke. He taught and treated me like a professional, and my self-esteem and skill soared. In only a short time, I was singing for weddings and the occasional classical gigs Fred sent my way. Often, they were jobs he was too busy to take. During the holiday season of my junior year, I won the tenor solo role in Handle's *Messiah*. We performed it at the San Jose Civic Auditorium. The rehearsals went without a hitch, and when the night of the performance came, I was loaded for bear. I got a haircut, shined my only pair of black shoes, and had my second-hand tuxedo cleaned and pressed. After dinner, I dressed and called a cab to take me to the auditorium. I arrived in plenty of time and was relieved when I finally was sitting on the stage listening to the crowd coming in to be seated. Being the first soloist to arrive, the others followed and sat on each side of me. I noticed that they greeted me a bit more whimsically than they had at the rehearsal the night before. The bass soloist, a distinguished English gentleman in his fifties, sat to my right and said, "Hello, young man." He was a fatherly type and a magnificent singer, receiving my complete respect. I would've been pleased even if he had addressed me as "young, drunken plumber."

I distinctly heard the alto soloist two chairs over snicker, and I thought I noticed a few folks in the front row laughing also. Then a horrible thought crept over me. Are my pants unzipped? Did I put my bow tie on upside-down? At that moment, the bass soloist, in his most articulate rolling voice, leaned over and spoke in my ear, "Nice socks, young man." I swallowed hard, bent forward, and looked down at my polished shoes from the corner of my better eye. In the bright glare of the floodlights, to my dismay, I discovered I was wearing the brightest, most garish pair of reddish-orange socks ever manufactured! I knew instantly that my roommate, Steve, had stuck them in my dress sock drawer as a joke. I thought for a minute about telling the truth to those around, but decided to quip to Mr. Walston, "Yessir, they'll help divert the audience's attention from all the mistakes I'm about to make!"

The Lord of badly dressed tenors was with me that night; my voice soared over the audience, and I remember the reverberation in the huge auditorium after singing the last note of my first aria *"Every Valley Shall be Exalted."* It was a magical night, and the genius of George Fredric Handel had allowed me to rise three feet above the stage floor.

20. Well, there it is!

To anyone who hasn't ever performed in front of a live audience, (of course, as a saxophonist friend of mine once said, "Who wants to perform in front of or behind, a dead one?) there are some gut-wrenchers that need to be explained. First, when you are an inexperienced performer, it's a good idea to be in relatively good health and physical condition. If you're not, there's a distinct possibility your adrenalin saturated heart will have to be beaten and stilled with a large mallet after you have died from lack of oxygen. This instant malady is often caused by massive milliliters of adrenalin slamming through your bloodstream at the sight of many expectant faces staring up at you wondering if you will be wonderful and spellbinding, or perhaps stink it up like a big dog!

No matter how prepared you might be or how confident you are with your skills and talents, when you walk out on that stage, you're as butt naked as the day you were born. When the day comes when this inner terror is no longer a factor, you better dig a big hole and dive into it or get a job as a bike messenger in San Francisco. For most competitive and proud performers, the backstage "shakes" isn't what many would think. They aren't from a fear or lack of faith in yourself, or fear that your efforts won't be accepted. The "shakes" are from the anticipation of rising to the already established heights you've set for yourself. However, I don't want to diminish the power of fear, for that emotion still hangs near the top of the endocrine hierarchy.

During the time I attended San Jose State University, it was necessary for all music performance students, regardless of major or minor, to perform in at least one departmental recital per semester, and for more advanced students, at least two performances. Once, for one of these jammed-packed recitals, I had prepared a beautiful aria from Puccini's *La Boheme*, titled: "Che Gelida Manina" and was waiting backstage for my turn to perform.

The young man who was to sing just before me was a police science major, with a music performance minor. I had met him a few times earlier while working out in the weight room of the venerable gym on the other side of campus. He was tall, at least six-five, and was a basketball player as well as a tight-end receiver on the university football team. Dressed in a sport coat and tie, he walked out on stage and stood near the crook of the open grand piano. He smiled at the audience and turned toward the accompanist, signaling her to begin the introduction to the German lieder song he was about to sing. I heard the familiar notes of Robert Schumann's "Ich Grolle Nicht" from *The Dichterliebe* song cycle begin to float out over the large room. I heard a distinct wheeze of breath being sucked in, and when the moment came for him to begin the first notes of the vocal there was nothing but silence. A low buzz of conversation rolled through the audience, and only seconds later, the business-like accompanist began the intro once more. Again, when the moment came for the athletic young man to sing, there was only another soft wheeze and silence. The next thing I heard was a communal gasp from the audience as the red-headed kid slowly sank to his knees on the floor, passing out for a few seconds from sheer terror.

21. Drunken Plumber's Last Ride

The end of my cycling experience and crap game of "when and where would it happen" took place on a cool fall evening during my sophomore year of college. Considering the thousands of miles I'd ridden over the last decade, I suppose I'd pushed the envelope as far as it could be stretched. I had been visiting a friend in Santa Clara, a city bordering San Jose, and had stayed most of the day and darkness was coming soon. She invited me to stay and she would fix dinner, but I knew better than to try and ride home in the dark. I said a reluctant good-bye and took off down West Hedding Street to go back across town to my shared apartment a mile or so from SJSU. The sun had just dipped behind the hills to the west, and because it was the weekend, there was little commuter traffic on the streets. The pavement had a gentle decline, and I was cruising along at a clip between twenty-five and thirty miles an hour. The passing traffic was moving slightly faster than I was riding.

At a signal light, I stopped beside a police car and was reminded of my ticket the year earlier. You know we hear about premonitions and the sense of impending danger? At that point, I began to feel those very same vibes. I slowed my pace a bit, and it probably saved my life. As I write this, sadly, a young science teacher in Marin County, just north of the Bay Area, lost his life only a month ago in the same conditions I'm about to describe.

As I've mentioned, there was little traffic, and as I approached another signal-controlled intersection, I noticed a dark sedan ahead pulling up to the left turn lane coming in the opposite direction. I thought I saw it come to a complete stop. My light was green, so I continued forward, not braking, but pedaling easier as I approached the crosswalk. I did something I'd learned to do years earlier and is a technique all cyclists who ride in traffic learn to do out of sheer survival.

I glanced quickly over my left shoulder to make sure that no one was going to make a right turn in front of me before the intersection. Many accidents are caused by this unfortunate motorist's move, for many drivers don't realize the cyclist's speed or mass. As I snapped my head back forward, to my horror, the dark car was accelerating, turning left into the intersection, heading directly at me. Obviously, the driver had not seen me in the shadows of the fading light. I crushed the brake handles of my Cinelli, but there was no way I could have stopped. There wasn't time to dump the bike, or even veer off to the right. When the driver finally saw me, the car's tires and brakes screeched, and with tremendous force, I struck the big sedan just behind the right front wheel-well. My beautiful Corsa disintegrated all over the intersection, as I flew forward over the handlebars. Please remember, on a road touring or racing bicycle, the seat is quite high, and the rider leans forward onto the downward-curving handlebars. As I flew over the hood of the car, I was already in the beginning of a forward somersault. I hit the windshield with such force it shattered, finished my forward roll, finally landing in a half-sitting position on the pavement ten feet from the opposite side of the car. Thanks to my Testa riding helmet I remained conscious, but nearly checked out for at least a minute or so. Another bit of sheer chance had helped me. When I'd left my friend's apartment, I had chosen to wear my riding gloves and the thick, padded coat that had protected me from the drizzle at seven that morning instead of attaching both items with a bungee to the small carrier at the rear of the Cinelli.

I remember not being able to breathe and not completely understanding what had just happened. The lady driving the car jumped out screaming, saying she was sorry and other things I just don't remember. I felt someone's hands on me and then saw the blurred mess of blood on my coat. It was very strange for I was still in a half-sitting position. My stomach muscles had obviously contracted and wouldn't allow my back to touch the pavement. I must have immediately gone into shock, for I felt little pain and the mixture of voices around me sounded surreal and coming from a long distance away. As weird as this sounds, I remember, as clearly as if it happened yesterday, seeing rivulets of red running down my exposed right calf, and with one hand, touching the mass of blood on the front of me. Quite detached, I marveled at how shiny and dark it looked on the light background of my coat. Someone kept asking if I was alright, but I don't think I could answer. Time was really messed up. I have no idea how long I sat on the street. Thankfully, my gut muscles eventually relaxed enough so that I could lay flat, and I remember finally being able to breathe better. Someone removed my helmet and strap, and the poor woman who had pulled in front of me came over but was still hysterical, so I think someone led her away. I do remember a man saying an ambulance was on its way.

One witness said I was almost upside-down when I hit the windshield directly in front of the driver. Most of the impact had been on my upper back and left side of my body. By some miracle, my head had only hit at an angle and had bounced off the hood or windshield because I only received a bloody nose and a good-sized lump on the left side of my face and jaw. Thank God I didn't hit the car straight on.

Two hours later in the emergency room, I again had my faith in that living God reaffirmed. The X-rays were all negative except for three hair-line cracks in the ribs on my left back. I had no broken bones or internal injuries. I suffered a mild concussion, but no other apparent head injuries. My nose was a blob of hamburger but wasn't broken. I had badly bruised my left hip, sprained and hyper extended the same knee (probably while summersaulting over the car), and deeply scarped the skin on the entire length of my right shin, having torn my pants from the knee to the ankle perhaps on the handlebars as I flew over them. I know today, had I been riding only a few miles an hour faster, I wouldn't have been as lucky. Or, as one of my smart-assed friends said, "If you had been riding faster, you would have already been past the damned intersection.

My Cinelli was salvageable, but very badly damaged. To repair it would be nearly as expensive as purchasing a nearly new one. The front forks and post were mangled, and the frame was badly bent and out of alignment. The lady who drove the car came to see me at the hospital, her insurance company later paid for the bike, and she was not cited. It wasn't negligence; she didn't see me because of the light and background. It was just an unfortunate accident that could have been far more tragic for both of us.

Talk about a wake-up call! I limped around with a walking cane for about three weeks and resigned myself to the glaring message: your days in the saddle are over, dude. After some of the things that happened to me while riding, you might think me certifiable but it's very difficult to explain. I still have to say it, "Thank you Cino Cinelli, your gorgeous creation gave me a taste of freedom I'll never forget!"

22. Just Another Mountain

A few years later at Jack London Square in Oakland, California, I auditioned for a new television program, "The All-American College Show." I suppose those today would say the show was too much rah-rah and plastic, but frankly after passing the audition I had a blast. The network flew me from the S.F. Bay Area to the Sony Studios in Burbank, CA, paying for everything. The producers, as is the practice of many shows today, filmed more than one show per day. The format was four acts of various soloists or groups, and at the end of the performances, a select panel of celebrity judges picked the winners. This was my first exposure to the "show biz" world, and I'd be a liar to say it didn't turn my head, as well as open my myopic eyes.

The experience was a "hello neophyte" for me, and I believe for some of the other performers as well. I remember after the first show seeing two young men who'd played guitar and sang, crouching in a corner of a dressing room, crying openly, having thought they'd won and learning they hadn't.

I was blown away by the big band arrangement they had made for me of the show tune "If I Ruled the World." They had built a fake mountain on which I would stand and sing, where, I suppose, I could "rule the world." Okay, I admit it was corny, but what did I know? They had dressed me in a rugged lumberjack outfit complete with axe. When my turn came for the judging, I was to stand on the mountain and acknowledge the applause. As my name was announced, I dutifully climbed Mt. Fuji, but couldn't see that the camera had zoomed in for a close-up. As the audience clapped, I bowed deeply, completely disappearing from the television screen. Dennis

James, the timeless host of the show, quipped on mic, "Looks like Paul Bunyan fell off the mountain!"

I gave it my best shot, and the audience seemed to love the song. But I soon learned a lasting lesson about the entertainment business when I was followed by a marvelously gifted young female singer who whispered her way through a well-known but noxious ballad. Her tiny voice lacked color and depth and wasn't always on pitch, but Ricky, my buddy who was playing trumpet on the second show, commented, "Man, ain't that the most sexy and totally stacked fox you've ever seen?!" Well, I said she was marvelously gifted. I came in second.

At the end of the show, all the contestants were to come out from off stage and stand in front of the studio audience while they clapped in appreciation.

The most memorable moment of that experience in Burbank was at the beginning of the filming for that day. I was taken totally by surprise when a tall, dark-haired man and his assistants entered the green room. I was the closest to the door when present Governor Ronald Reagan shook my hand as I stood! He'd just finished filming an intro to the show, making a short statement about the audience seeing another side of the "college protest scene" (which at that time was taking up so much of the media coverage). He remarked that the students on the show represented another facet of current campus life.

Later on, I would listen to his intro with much interest, but at the time, I was a Democrat and had not heard many things said in a positive nature about Ronnie from any of my liberal friends and fellow musicians. I can say without reserve, he was the warmest, most concerned politician (or public figure for that matter) I have ever met. He sent his staff out of the green room and sat down and talked to the entire group with genuine interest and open-mindedness. One of the college contestants, a tall young man with a beard and shaved head, asked in an aggressive voice something about Mr. Reagan's position on the Vietnam conflict. His response was to the effect, "We're all Americans. We need to support those in harm's way, and of course respect and listen to each other's opinions, no matter what our personal views."

On my way home the next evening, I walked into a lounge in the L.A. airport carrying my second-place trophy in my carry-on, strangely feeling the compelling need for an adult refreshment. I always had a difficult time entering a dark or dimly lit room from the bright light outside, but I soon fumbled into a barstool along the right side of the room. A fantastic piano player was tearing it up in the corner. A few minutes later, a young GI from Georgia came in and sat down next to me and ordered a beer. We soon took up a conversation, and he said he was headed for Saigon, that his training was disarming ordinance and removing land mines. I remember saying a silent prayer for the young soldier. I had another hour before my flight left for Oakland, and in the ensuing conversation, I explained my meteoric military career and the vision thing. Our conversation eventually got around to music. He described to me the African American pianist who continued to play without stopping for a break. Each song seemed tastier than the last. "Yessir", the young GI said. "He looks to be at least eighty or so, and I bet he don't weigh more than a hundred-thirty pounds. The amazin' thing is he don't move his body a lick while runnin' all over those keys. He just looks straight ahead with his eyes closed."

I told the GI I'd give my left whatever to play like that. After a couple more liquid sandwiches, including a shot of Wild Turkey, which the young GI insisted on buying, I thought it best I retire from the premises while I was still capable of remaining upright while walking. The soldier walked out with me, and when we passed the old man, I asked the GI to show me where the pianist's tip jar was. He did, and I tossed in the dollars I had left, wishing I could afford more. I had to talk to the old man. "Excuse me sir," I said, "but you have to be the best stride-style piano player I've heard since records of 'Fats' Waller or Art Tatum. How can you play like that, with all that energy in your music, and never move a muscle in the rest of your body?"

The old man ripped an ascending blues line that made me nearly drop my jaw, then replied in a slow Mississippi drawl, a line I'll remember the rest of my life. "Baby, I give ya some advice. When you goin' no place…you might as well go slow!" As time passed and my eyesight continued to decrease, the classical jobs and opportunities became scarcer. I was continually frustrated that despite my good voice, directors and agents quickly lost interest in hiring me as soon as they found my vision was so poor and that I could no longer read music. Over time I've learned to understand their reasoning but not to agree.

The biggest bone of contention is the ability (or lack of it) of the blind performer to see the conductor for cues. What many blockheaded and narrow-minded conductors don't realize is that blind musicians often possess a tremendous sense of tonal memory and sensitivity, often coupled with an increased capacity of memorization skills, making them a definite asset to an ensemble situation, and certainly as a solo performer. The fact that the blind performer is unable to see the conductor's eyes or baton for cues is often more of an ego aggravator to the conductor, than a detractor to the performance. On that note, I'll climb down my mountain and bury my axe.

The second issue is the blind musician's lack of mobility, and inability to read music scores and lead sheets. Modern assistive music braille technology has put an end to this print music concern. I soon found that the only way I could make a living for my new family and myself while still remaining in music was to switch to playing jazz and pop music and teaching. Considering some of the other means of gainful employment I attempted in the interim, these were not unpleasant options.

To this day, I have the utmost respect for the folks across our country who work with the strength of their hands and backs. For nearly four years, I worked different jobs while finishing college part-time and trying to play music. I worked as a night dispatcher for a large trucking firm, keeping the position of the trucks and their various trailers scattered around California which I memorized from my helper's descriptions. I could barely read half the information on the lading chart board. It was the first of only two jobs in my life where I was "canned". After six months on the job, I sent a big rig all the way to L.A. with the wrong trailer for the shipment. The bummer was, I know I screwed up, but I'm sure the driver knew he had the wrong equipment. Somewhere along the line I must have pissed him off.

I then went to work at a local food cannery, and in a month was promoted from the cannery to the lithographing department of their can manufacturing plant, handling thousands of three foot by three sheets of razor-sharp tinplate every graveyard shift. The following year, most of the new hires (me included) were laid off, as the frozen food industry made its inroads into sales. For one summer, I ran a raw bone grinding machine for horse carcasses, grinding the bones into meal. This pungent job was at a well-known pet food company. That summer I found gaining weight was not a problem, I usually "tossed my cookies" every morning before the first break, and seldom could eat lunch! I know how lucky I was. Being around so much machinery, I was never seriously injured, though I did manage to wriggle out of some hairy close calls.

23. He's Totally Gone Down the Tubes!

In the winter of that year I was engaged to my first wife, Barbara. We were married just months later, and soon had a daughter on the way. I didn't realize it at the time, but Barbara's medical future was bleak, and there were some hellatious peaks ahead for both of us to scale.

A year after my daughter was born, though my sight had diminished even more, Floyd got me a job with the construction outfit he worked with in Alameda, California. Alameda is a beautiful island on San Francisco Bay, about seven miles by three in size. I never would have imagined I would come close to getting killed there, and then be living there thirty years later. The city had just built a new section of the island, filled in by sand dredged from the bay. Later, the company I worked for as a laborer was assigned the task of laying all the underground sewer and storm drain systems for this new section of the island. Work moved along, and at the end of the summer I was making such good money I decided to continue and go back to school part time at night. I was only one of two Caucasian men on the labor crew and learned volumes about working with others.

We'd only recently built the sand streets and concrete curbs, connecting the street storm drain openings with the large underground concrete storm drainpipes we'd laid earlier that year. The lots for future buildings were open fields of sand. That year, the rain came early and wouldn't stop. It became everyone's nightmare. On one terribly stormy weekend, tons of sand washed into the storm drains and clogged up most of the pipes below ground. I was part of the crew assigned to begin cleaning them out as soon as the weather cleared enough for us to work. We took high-pressure hoses down inside the manholes, blasting the sand into central areas where it could be then pulled up by pumps the pumps above. This worked with minimal success, for we were only moving the sand around. A foreman decided to put large inflatable plugs into the huge pipes at various locations to keep the sand from moving into that section, while the neighboring section was being cleaned— sounded like it would work.

On one bone-freezing morning after another three days of rain, I arrived to work with wind from an Alaskan front blowing rain in off the bay. The foreman was asking for a volunteer to go down a deep manhole to remove one of the plugs. Extra pay was involved so I decided my services were needed immediately. I was loaded into a van and told to put on a latex wet suit dusted in talcum. That's when I learned the plug was underwater! Pressure up the line had filled the interior of the manhole to the top. When we arrived at the site of my impromptu water ballet, a weight belt and sturdy nylon rope were tied around my waist. Two other workers far less inspired by amassing capital assets would man the rope. I was to hold my breath and climb down the metal rebar ladder inside the wall of the interior of the buried concrete manhole. A good description of one of these things would be a fifteen-foot tall concrete affair shaped much like a huge thermos bottle. The manhole cover you see on the street level would be the cap or lid, and the pipes entering it underground would connect to the bottle near its base. Of course, the whole contraption is buried below the street. I was assured someone had already climbed down into the manhole a few hundred yards away, checking to see if water was in the hole. The boss said not to worry, there was water behind the plug I was about to remove. The pressure should be equal on both sides. All I had to do was let a little air out of the plug, pull it from the pipe opening, and bring it to the surface.

Having been known to swim large lakes in Oklahoma, I thought it would be a quick buck. Surprise, surprise. Holding my breath, I scurried down the submerged ladder on the inside wall, and in the blackness, quickly found the plug and its pressure valve. With the gadget they'd given me, I began to let the air out. The bubbles screamed and hissed as they passed my face and headed for the surface. Suddenly, I felt the plug move— not much, but a definite movement. I remember thinking, "that's not right." There was a sudden loud pop, and the plug disappeared from my hand. In a split second I was pulled into the entrance of the now open pipe, as the dirty water was pulled into it. I grabbed for the edge of the rebar ladder but was too late. As I banged into the opening of the pipe, I tried to catch the edge of it where it entered the manhole, but the pressure of the rushing water was much too strong for me to hold on to the smooth surface of the concrete.

Down the pipe I went! Silently I prayed the guys upstairs weren't thumbing through a "Playboy" or taking a smoke break and were holding on to the rope firmly. If not, I knew I was history. Then, there was a tremendous jerk as I came to the end of the slack section of the rope. I'd gone in feet first and could still feel the water rushing by my body as the rope cut into the flesh of my waist above the weight-belt and pants of the wet suit. It seemed an eternity until the water finally stopped moving past me. Then, I felt the rope being frantically pulled from above. I was running out of oxygen, but I knew the only way I'd make it was to not panic and fight the help from above. As if I was a hooked sturgeon, I popped out of the pipe, and seconds later broke surface, gasping for air. Chuck, the foreman, said later I'd been underwater for over a minute and a half, but it seemed like the time was equivalent to a career.

We learned later that there must've been a large section of the pipe not filled with water, the sand having plugged it from each end. When I popped the plug, the water pressure from the line behind me rushed in to fill the now open area, taking me with it. Minutes later, I was sitting in the company owner's trailer, hot towels wrapped around me, drinking a huge cup of warm whiskey, flavored with a shot of coffee. I was driven home early, and for weeks was treated by the foremen and other workers as if I was some kind of hero. I thought, "no hero, maybe a little greedy and very lucky." Remember, if you have someone on the job you can't stand, when he least expects it, give him a plug!

I learned many valuable and lasting lessons about working with others, and personal respect for those around me, from those experiences with our hard workers. In retrospect, though I know times have changed, where else but in America could someone with a disability make enough money to support a wife, daughter, and newborn son, yet still manage to scrape enough together to finish college? Man is that why everybody seems to want to come here!

24. Mother Gaylord

After the construction job closed down, I experienced a period of six months or so when my remaining sight opted for early retirement. I lost at least half of what remained, so I decided before I became an obituary statistic, it was time to devote myself to learning the skills needed to be a success in the music business. A wonderful man from whom I'd bought guitar strings and picks for years gave me a job in his music studio and store. The pay was less than half what I'd been making in construction, so I needed a second income. I learned of an opening in a popular lounge band, and though I'd never played in a professional pop group before, I knew it was a chance to make some extra money and practice what I loved most. Early one evening a few days later, after an intensive audition with the leader of the band, I attended my first rehearsal with "Daybreak."

The soundproofed studio off the house was a riot of intermingled smells and general chaos. Small children scurried around the room, all products of different band members or relatives of Joey, the keyboardist and bandleader. "Somebody come and get the trolls outta here," he shouted. "We've gotta get started. The bride and her mother are gonna show up in a half hour to hear the band." I rarely felt comfortable in strange groups, and on that day, I felt even more uneasy and nervous. As Mark, the electric bass player was tuning up, Joey asked, "Have any of you guys heard from Gaylord? He knows how important this gig is. The groom is the mayor's son!" We began the rehearsal, and twenty minutes later, I heard a great banging and crashing coming from the screen and front door of the house.

Phil, the drummer, laughed loudly and announced, "It's either an earthquake or big Gare." I felt the floor vibrate from the big man's weight as he approached the door to the rehearsal room. He burst onto the scene with all the grace and subtlety of Attila the Hun.

"Damn-it Gaylord, you're late again. What's the story this time?" I heard the frustration and anger in Joey's voice, but Gaylord didn't answer. The disruption continued as he found his customary place in the room.

"Come on maestro, chill out. I made it," he boomed. There was a rustling from a paper bag he'd brought with him, and then the snap and scent of a beer can being opened. I heard him assembling his sax as he said, "There was a bunch of little kids down the street when I pulled up a while ago. They were trying to throw a football, but they were doing it all wrong, so my man, I had to offer some coaching advice. It was my duty as a caring and responsible citizen."

Joey let out a sigh of resignation before speaking, "Gary, put that can behind the amp, the people will be here any time now. Come on over here, I want you to meet a great guitarist and singer. Roy can't see very much, but he can really tear it up on the guitar. Roy Wayne, this organism is Gary Gaylord. He's our tenor sax man and all-around screw-up."

"Ah, Sir Joseph," Gary teased, "you wouldn't talk so cocky if you were a foot taller and didn't sign the checks." As I reached out and shook Gary's huge right paw, my hand felt as though it had disappeared halfway up to my elbow. I was six feet, weighed 180, and had been lifting heavy weights regularly, but at that moment, I felt about as intimidating as Winnie the Pooh. I could feel his mass before me, his voice was coming from about six feet four or five, and every time he took a breath and rumbled to speak, it seemed a good part of the air in the room disappeared. He laughed, then roared, "Hey alright, a honky Stevie Wonder that picks guitar. It's about time we got some real talent in this pitiful damned outfit." Being so defensive about my sight, I'll always remember the feelings I felt at that moment: anger, a little embarrassment, and more than anything else an instant dislike for the big, blustering musician who'd be standing on stage with me for the next six and a half years.

Up until the day I met him, my advancing loss of sight was still a sensitive subject. Even into my late twenties, like so many others with similar problems, I'd always tried to conceal my poor vision. I hated the stigma of people thinking I had a flaw or weakness of some kind. "Big Gary" was about to change my outlook forever. From that first rehearsal, my attitude began to change. It had to or I wouldn't have survived.

He was blunt and relentless, quickly dubbing me "The Moth," for with my night blindness and remaining light perception; whenever the band took a break, I always seemed to gravitate to the light. Every time Gary would jab me with one of his teasing wisecracks, I'd bite my lip and do a slow burn. Soon, I had to admit that some of his off-the-wall quips were dry, always rude, but at the moment, very funny (even though I often was the subject of the jab). One weekend, we were late for a gig, and I was helping unload the van. While carrying both the heavy P.A. speaker columns, I asked if one of the guys could lead the way up the steps into the reception hall. Gary quickly stepped in front of me and announced loudly in a mock feminine voice, "Come on, my little Sweetness. Follow Mother Gaylord." I began to laugh. Soon I was laughing so hard, I had to put the speakers down to get my breath. Gary's timing was as sharp as his ribald humor.

Some months later, I walked off the edge of a sidewalk going into a private golf club in Pleasanton, California, pitching headfirst into a large bunch of shrubs next to the sidewalk. Some members of the club came running to my assistance, but Gary (who could see I was okay) quipped, "The jackass got himself into it without any help, so he can probably get himself out!" After the job that day, Gary threatened to tie me to his belt with a rope, to keep me from going astray. "We can't lose you, Dinkus," he said, "these other yahoos aren't nearly as much fun to jerk around."

As time passed, I learned to put up with his constant ribbing, being called every nickname imaginable: Larry Load, Stevie Blunder, Ray (in reference to Ray Charles). Slowly I began to understand what Gary's teasing was all about. In his own unrefined way, he was making me take a lighter attitude toward my disability whether I liked it or not. By the end of my first year with the band, I knew big Gare's teasing and raucous personality were simply shields. As long as he was the center of attention with his clowning around, he was safe. No one could get close or force him to reveal his true emotions. Yet. under the bravado, he had a truly gentle side. He loved kids, and spent hours teaching my young son, Tony, to ride a bike and throw and catch a football. My eight-year-old daughter Julie loved him and called him the "big bear with a beard."

Gary was a captivating showman on stage. He played the sax like he lived, hard and fast, and there was never a doubt who was the audience's favorite when Gary took a driving solo. As the years passed, we became quite close friends, but outside the band, his single lifestyle, and my responsibilities to raising a family gave us little time or activities in common.

After I left the band, we gradually lost touch. Recently, I tried to find where he's living now but had no success. If he walked into the room this moment, I'd give "Mother Gaylord" a warm Italian hug, thank him, and again shake his big hand. There are many that could never forgive his seeming insensitivity to me (and to others for that matter), but in truth, his heart was bigger than my ego. Playing music with Gary and the other band members on those wild and wonderful nights in the clubs helped make me less self-centered, and a more tolerant teacher and father. It's amazing how thin our protective armor becomes when someone sees past our first line of protection, the defensiveness of our own insecurity.

25. On the Road Again

The band Daybreak taught me "people skills" that will remain with me forever and certainly was a vehicle for some good laughs and lessons. Big Gare had a terrible habit of losing his band paycheck, often even before getting home the same evening. We'd been playing at a fine restaurant and nightclub on a pier on San Francisco Bay. Its nickname to those who were regulars, was "The Tuna" (The owner preferred The Blue Dolphin). For years, we played there for three nights a week, and on Saturday nights Joey, the bandleader, would give us our checks. These stipends often included money for any weddings or casuals we'd played that week.

After the third set, Joey was helping me off stage to take our break when he looked over and saw Gare's check hanging off an amplifier, his car keys on top of it. "Roy Wayne, I'm gonna fix that big ape! I'm getting tired of voiding checks and writing him new ones two days later." He wrapped the check around the keys and dropped them into the bell of Gary's tenor sax, which was sitting on a stand to the right of the stage. Of course, Mother Gaylord was already at the bar in the process of getting refreshed.

Our last set was always the loudest and most energetic, for we played dance music and the latest rock and pop tunes. Big Gare was literally blowing his brains out. The keys in the bottom of the bell had thrown his horn out of tune, and he couldn't understand why he was having to blow so hard. After the second song, he turned to me and cursed, saying he wanted me to have the repairman at the music store where I worked fix the damn thing. You must understand, this six-foot-five, nearly three-hundred-pound man was as mechanical as a bar of soap. He continued cussing and blowing for the next half-hour, and as the night went on, Joey and I could hardly keep from laughing every time Gare played a lead line.

At the end of Gary's driving solo in a Carlos Santana Latin rock, he heard something rattle in his horn. Shaking his Selmer Mark Six and then tipping it upside down, he watched the car keys hit the floor. In the same moment, the now damp check floated onto the dance floor! Phil, the drummer, nearly fell off his stool when he saw the startled expression on the big man's face as Gare roared, "Who's the !$^* clown?"

Joey the rooster quipped, "Looks like we're lookin' at him!" As I remember, Big Gare didn't lose any more checks.

26. Are you playing with the flour children?

One of the great perks of playing music with a good band is the great casuals you always pick up by word of mouth, and from the boxes of business cards given out over hundreds of jobs. I know some of the cards we gave to folks slept in their wallets and purses for years until someone got married, remarried, divorced again and re-remarried, bar mitzvahed, or eventually waked, canonized, or sainted. These casual jobs always paid better than the steady club gigs but weren't as dependable as steady income. I think the romance of the casual was the relaxed settings, and the fact you never knew quite what to expect when you showed up to play. The Daybreaks, as we were often called to our dismay, was fortunate. We were booked many months ahead at the local Officers' Clubs at the military bases, and at most of the larger halls and community centers. Most often, they were for wedding receptions or dances, with an occasional anniversary thrown in for variety.

High in the Oakland hills is a beautiful area known as Knowland Park. Perched on the top of the hills, is the "Snow Building" (often rented out for weddings), and we played there dozens of times over the years. One gig in particular was one I'll never to forget. We arrived early in the afternoon to set up our equipment on the stage. The hall manager let us in and muttered, "Be careful of the damned brush in the vases all over the place. These hippies are some kind of ecology nuts," as he disappeared into the kitchen.

"The decorations are really stark," said Joey as he helped me to my usual spot in front of the drums. "All the tables are covered with some kind of green and brown paper, and the flowers look like something you dried to stuff a mattress." We went about our business getting the band together, worrying as usual if Phil the drummer would show up in his "band" outfit (or the jeans and sneakers he usually wore). Over many a season, we heard every excuse known to man why he couldn't wear his band uniform that day: the damned cat peed in the dryer, and I couldn't wash and dry my pants; I loaned my shirt to my roommate and the jerk threw up on it; I had to use my white belt for a tourniquet for a circus sword swallower who got the hiccups; I broke the zipper on my fly when a cop drove up, as I took a pause next to the car on the way home last night at two in the morning; a freakin' eagle swooped down from nowhere and stole my white desert boot, while that Tibetan princess was giving me a foot massage. You name it, we heard it.

The Blue Men had nothing on us. At that time in the old music biz, it was very fresh to be dressed exactly alike. Perhaps with that philosophy, nobody really knew which one of the clowns playing on stage made that horrific clam (a clam is the old musician's term for a wrong note or mistake). It's taken me years to finally get to the point I can eat the hard-shelled little critters without breaking out in a sweat!

Guests slowly began to fill up the place, and big Gare commented on how casual everyone was dressed, and why in hell did we have to wear our dress outfits. In minutes, the smell of high-grade marijuana filled the room from every opening in the place, and we knew it was going to be an interesting afternoon. We should have known what to expect from the bride and groom's request for "Come Together" by the Beatles as their first song. The lyrics of that song always fascinated me, and after all these years, I'm still trying to figure out what exactly is "toe-jam football." Soon a couple of large kegs of draft beer were brought in and the fun began. The guys in the band said everyone, men and women alike, were draining large pint paper cups of the plentiful brew with reckless abandon, often chasing it with ample shots from pint bottles of "Yukon Jack" whiskey. Of course, our illustrious band members were above such debauchery and abstained religiously.

We started playing some soft rock and the noise level in the place began rising to warp twelve. Within forty-five minutes, I could hear the party was taking on all the salient indications of an impending train wreck. Soon there was much howling and hooting as the bride and groom arrived in a road-weary Dodge van. I found out later that it was decorated with enough graffiti to keep a clean-up paint crew busy for the next two weeks. We finally took a break and started to grab some of the food laid out on long tables off to the side of the hall. But when we got there, Joey said it looked like somebody's little brother had run a weed eater through the food platters, so I decided to pass on the "fingered" finger food and live to pick another day. Perhaps another of Mrs. Kelly's quality control tests on the draft beer was called for on my part. Then, to my surprise, I heard the wedding coordinator talking to Joey and telling him the wedding ceremony was about to be performed right there in the building! We'd all assumed the wedding had already taken place somewhere else.

I'm relating the visual descriptions second-hand, but I swear the details are accurate. When the bride and groom entered the room, the guests crowded around them and a great lot of kissing, hugging, cross-checking, and scrums were shared by all. Many "peaces" and "loves" echoed through the room, and I heard Joey cracking up next to me right in the middle of a tune. When we finished, he leaned over and told me the bride was dressed in a beautiful wedding gown complete with short train. Nothing unusual and certainly lovely, but she was wearing no makeup, no bra, and no shoes. Her long-haired groom made an instant hit in his tuxedo. His tie was tied perfectly, and his cummerbund snugly fastened around his middle. Fine you say, what's wrong with this picture? He wore no shirt, socks, or shoes and sported a woven headband around flowing hair past his shoulders. Both prospective newly-weds wore no jewelry.

The ceremony soon unfolded in a muddle of poetry and readings, having something to do with freedom, sharing, and respect of each other's individuality, something akin to "Let's get married, baby, so we can both be free individuals and do whatever the hell we want, okay?" One young man actually told the groom he expected him to share his new bride. Of course, I assumed he was joking, but now in retrospect, I'm not really sure.

The crowd got noisier, we got louder, the beer flowed faster, and George our new bass player said he never saw so many bare breasts through loose body wraps and shawls in his life. The gig ended being a knockdown, drag-out, rock and roll dance orgy, complete with a few strippers, hash smokers, and I'm overwhelmed to think what other drugs and illegal substances were being consumed in and out of the building. But I'm sure if any narc officer would have wandered in that afternoon, he'd have thrown up his hands in terror, and in a fit of self-preservation hopped the next flight south. Sometime later, the bride and groom left the premises in a rain of wild and brown rice, and the party immediately went down the proverbial toilet. Soon, a couple of fights broke out, one in the men's room and another outside on the patio. Shortly thereafter, another on the dance floor. None of us were really surprised when the power went off. "Turn out the lights, the party's over," big Gare began singing as he put away his horn, and we quickly began moving our equipment down the back stairs of the stage. Joey had already taken the check for the show from the bride's father, and it was time to hook it for other parts of town. We all had to admit later, for a bunch of followers and disciples of "The Summer of Love," we supplied the musical fuel for one of the finest brawls in years.

27. There She Blows!

Back at The Tuna, my favorite set of music was the third. We always played a lot of jazz swing and dance standards with some catchy Brazilian tunes thrown in. We had many regulars in the crowd, and one couple in particular were fantastic dancers. It was somewhat unusual, for both were immense people. Both would give big Gare a run for his money at the midnight buffet aboard any cruise ship! We'd just finished an up-tempo boogie tune when the couple went to their usual table to get their breath. The chairs were leather and very plush, and Joey said when the guy's wife sat down, she leaned back, really wiped out.

We started the intro to an old swing classic someone had requested, Glenn Miller's "In the Mood," when the husband (who was still standing) grabbed his lady's hand and tried to pull her up out of the chair. As stout as she was, the big man was tugging mightily, leaning back for leverage. Her wrists must've been perspiring, for as he gave one more prodigious pull, his hands broke free from hers and he fell backward toward the stage. He carried too much ballast on board to stop his precarious progress and plowed full tilt into the bandstand. Without even a perfunctory "hello" as he passed, he flew by my right between Gary and me, clearing out both our microphone stands at the same time. General Sherman's march to the sea was abruptly stopped when he met solid resistance from the flank. The reverb unit inside my Fender Twin Reverb amp roared out into the room with enough racket to awaken any drunk asleep on the throne in the restroom. The six-foot speaker column of the P.A. tipped backward and fell against the huge plate glass windows circling the lounge. The windows provided customers a fabulous view of the bay. Even with the chaos around me, I remember hearing the thump and the strange does it make?" She bent down and picked up another, tossed it into the surf and said, "It makes a difference to that one!"

sound of the vibrating glass, as it decided whether to shatter into the bay or live to fight another dance. I immediately had nightmarish visions of big Gare in his usual late-night painless condition, floundering away in the water, with Joey barking commands, both wearing ill-fitting wet suits, yelling at each other trying to fish our P.A. from Neptune's Galley. The big man jumped to his feet and retraced his steps to the point of attack, never saying a word to any of us. Later, he left a large wad of bills in the tip jar, and within minutes a round of adult beverages arrived at the bandstand.

28. Up Scale

Playing and entertaining is not only performing, but also working with the people. Untold thousands of great talents have gone by the wayside due to their inability to work well and interact with fellow musicians or their public. One of the greatest electric jazz bassists that ever played was shot and killed in an argument with a club owner after the place had closed for the night. Without respect for your backers and public, you might as well go "dig clams" for a living. But, even the most tolerant and saintly performer occasionally gets some clown who drives him up, or possibly through, the proverbial wall.

Ours was the brother of the Musicians Union's business agent, who brought a group of loud-mouthed and obnoxious drunks to the club at least once a month. This "lounge lizard" always walked into the place like he was "the artist formerly known as Prince," and expected everyone to move aside. He once asked some older customers to get up and move; they were sitting at his "favorite" table. In the years we played at the "Tuna," his was the only group the manager ever asked to leave because of their foul language near the dining room and dance floor. Another bad habit this class act had (when his wife wasn't looking), was fondling waitress' bottoms or any other malleable surface available. Two of the club's best female servers wouldn't wait on his table for that very reason. After a few rounds of drinks to get his ego stoked, he'd descend on the band and demand (not ask) to sing a few songs. This was something we allowed others to do frequently, especially when one of our fellow musicians was in town or between gigs.

But you must believe me, this guy, we'll call him Lance (his last name was English I believe, Boyle or something like that), had a voice like a cross between a gas-powered leaf blower and Louis Armstrong. Actually, my apologies to Louis. He was Pavarotti next to Sir Boyle. He'd always grab either Gare's or my mic and start jawing to the crowd, usually in the middle of a tune when we couldn't stop him. Big Gare said he didn't try to head him off, because he always enjoyed the coming "gong show." There always followed a couple of racist or crude jokes, at which his friends laughed hysterically. Then, without warning he'd break into some song without giving us a clue what it was, or what key it was in.

Joey and I would softly follow him and play a few chords until we'd figured out the key, and then yell it to the other guys in the band. When he finished a song, he'd jump right into the next in the same fashion. I couldn't see Joey our bandleader, but I knew he was smoldering. He was a wiry Italian and had a short fuse anyway. To add to our grief, the head cocktail server came up to Joey, and said the boss wanted us to let "Torrid Tonsils" continue. His car dealer friend had just bought a round for the entire lounge, more than a hundred people. We were a lot younger and cockier then, and when the time came for his big finale ("For The Good Times, the timeless old country classic), Joey leaned over and whispered to me and George, the bass player, "Jack this sucker up a whole step at the end of every chorus." Gleefully, we followed our leader's instructions, and Lance baby had no choice but to follow the band as we moved steadily into higher and higher keys. By the end of the song, the audience was laughing, the head bartender (who was not one of Lance's admirers) was jeering openly, and our country crooner was sounding as if his privates had been squeezed in a vice.

After Joey amputated the angry canary's microphone, Lance informed us that we all would soon be out of a job, because the headwaiter was dating his sister, and his brother ran the union where we'd never get another gig. We were informed that all of us were nothing more than the other word for posterior body orifices, and the owner of the place would hear about his poor treatment. Gary had heard enough, and not fancying himself in any way to be one of those lowly physiological phenomena, rudely ushered the "Velvet Frog" from the bandstand. Nearly a month later to the day, undaunted by fear of defeat, Sir Boyle stumbled on stage and snatched a mic. To this day, I can't figure out what his sister dating the headwaiter had to do with the possibility of us getting canned!

29. Lookin' a Little Pale There, Pilgrim!

Not long after the band stopped playing the clubs, I decided to start working as a single act. I thought male nude dancing was definitely not in the picture, because with my lack of vision, it was quite possible I could easily walk off the stage, and then I wouldn't be wearing any clean underwear when they took me to the hospital. Stand-up comedy was beginning to be very popular, and from my last quip, you can see I didn't have enough material to do a night's gig. I must admit, there's still a bundle of blind jokes I get a kick out of telling:

An industrious, young, blind fellow worked at a fruit stand. He was great. He could tell the condition and age of fruits and vegetables by their feel and scent and could guess the weight of items within an ounce, just by holding them in his hand. He was really helpful moving crates around 'cause he was strong as a bull. One afternoon, an elderly gentleman came in and asked him, "Young man, can you sell me half a cantaloupe?"

The blind fellow stammered for a second, and then said, "Sir, I'm terribly sorry, but that's impossible. The seeds and goop inside would make a terrible mess. The old man persisted, "I haven't tasted cantaloupe for at least a year, and I only have enough money for a half."

"Hey man, that's alright," the young man said. "I'll pay for the rest."

"Oh no," he said, "I have my pride, what would my friends say if they found out I took charity from a blind guy?"

A little exasperated, the young man made it back to the boss' office, knocked, and stuck his head in the door. "Hey Mr. Lucca. There's some old fart outside that wants to buy a half a cantaloupe." As soon as he said it, he heard the old man cough right behind him. Quickly he added, "And this fine gentleman would like to buy the other half."

That evening at closing time, Mr. Lucca told the young man to come in his office. He said, "Larry, I saw the way you handled that cantaloupe deal today, and I gotta say you think fast on your feet. You've worked really hard for me these last few years, and I think it's time you had a little reward. I'm in the process of building the newest and best produce mart in Canada, right in downtown Calgary. I want you to go up there and be my produce manager. How 'bout it?"

"Ah, no way boss," the young man pleaded, "all they got in Calgary are hookers and hockey players."

Lucca blurted, "Damn-it young man, you watch your mouth. I'll have you know my wife's from Calgary!"

"Oh, yeah? That's trippy, Joe. Which team she play for?"

I continued playing solo jobs and had learned to play the bass pedals with my feet (these are like the pedals on a church organ), and using a neck holder, played blues harmonica while playing the guitar. Later on, with a good drum machine, I made a pretty passable one-man band. You must realize what a change it was going from classical music to pop and country and jazz. Think of the challenge of singing Paul Simon's "Fifty Ways to Love Your Leaver," and not have it sound like "Celeste Aida" by Verdi. It's amazing how quickly we adapt when we're hungry.

My biggest problem, as always, was getting around and moving equipment, a musician's eternal task. A friend of mine had an uncle who booked bands and singles for lounge work. He heard me in the bar of one of the local dinner houses and charmed me into believing I was the second coming of Christ to the music world. You would think by then I'd have more sense, but I immediately put my teaching on hold, invested my monumental savings into dot com stocks, and headed for the romance of being "on the circuit." For the next twelve weeks, six nights a week, it seemed I played every sleazy lounge, butt hut, and beer joint in the east bay area. All the gigs of course were booked by my "mentor/agent" for a "nominal" percentage of the fee.

My last weekend of this whirlwind tour was in the old cowboy town of Pleasanton at the aging and historic Pleasanton hotel. I'd played at the Hotel many times in years past with the band. A terrible storm had hit the area that weekend, and the temperature was below freezing outside. It was a Friday, but the dining room was nearly deserted, and at the bar, I think we served a grand total of ten customers the entire night, not counting the grizzly old bartender and me. I was busily picking away at my uninspiring set of cover tunes and current pop hits, doing my best to sound as close to the recording as possible. It took me years to learn this method wasn't where it's at. No matter how well you imitate someone, and even if you're a better musician, you're never going to be as good as the original. Better to do their music in your own hopefully unique style.

Somewhere around midnight, someone came in, jangling and with boots clomping. I heard the man's gravelly voice at the bar and continued my dutiful minstreling, oblivious of his presence. After about three more songs, he stomped up to the stage. This guy was big Gary's twin brother, only taller. As soon as he spoke, I could hear he was as tall as I was, and I was on the high stage! The bartender told me later he wore a wide brimmed hat and one of those sheepskin jackets with a wide collar (that as a kid, I always saw the cowboys in Montana wear on TV).

He started talking, and he had my attention, "Hey long-hair, in the inside pocket of this here coat, I got a loaded Smith & Wesson." I'm glad I couldn't see his face as he growled on, "Son, I've heard 'bout all that rock and roll hippie sh—. I c'n take. You best start pickin' some country music." The old bartender must've looked up at that moment as I stopped right in the middle of the pop tune I was playing and whipped into Willie Nelson's "Blue Eyes Cryin' in the Rain."

30. Searching for Twin Peaks

Later, I worked for five years for another restaurant chain, The Prime Rib Inns. Here's a tip to all you struggling musicians. If you want to insure you've got a gig in a great place for a long time, teach the owner's wife to sing a few tunes. With some arm bending I talked Lou Jay, a virtuoso electronic accordionist, into forming a duo. I sang show tunes, did impressions, played trumpet, banjo, and guitars, while he filled the entire Western Hemisphere with his Lovell custom-made organ squeezebox. Lou actually had a gold solo album with Capitol Records. We called our act "ShowTime." Though some did say it was an unnatural act, it was a tremendous success, and for years the lounge at the club was standing room only. I wish I could say it was due to my marvelous wit and stellar vocal talents, but in truth, Lou was one of the finest showmen I've ever had the pleasure of working with.

I was still trying to face the fact that, by now, I was nearly totally blind. Looking back, it would have been so much easier if I'd bit the bullet and used a long cane, but hey man, this was show biz! I had it down to a science. Every table in the place was the same size with a candle in the center. Out of the corner of my left eye, I could see the lights behind the bar, and knew the placement of every piece of furniture in the place. You wouldn't believe the number of restrooms I memorized over a space of thirty-five years. Shirley, a very pretty and bright older server, would always help me from the stage whenever she was available, and Lou would often do the same.

One night after "ShowTime," I needed to replace a string on one of my guitars and ended up on the stage alone. When finished, I moved forward and knew exactly how I'd get to the bar from the lights of the candles on the tables. What I didn't know was, during the show, customers had moved their chairs around into the normal walkways to get a better view of the stage. I stepped down off the sixteen-inch high stage and, as always, extended my hands a little in front of me to feel for obstacles. I figured out later in my life, this probably looked far more bizarre than using a cane ever would. To anyone who didn't know I had a vision problem, I probably looked stoned or drunk most of the time. I'd only taken a few steps when both hands made contact with something warm and fuzzy. I later found I'd accomplished something I couldn't have replicated in a thousand tries. However, now that I think of it, the attempts would have been far more fun than a root canal. A woman and her husband had been sitting directly in front of the stage, and after the show, they'd stayed in their seats finishing their drinks in silence, then decided to claim their reservation for dinner in the dining room. The poor woman was nearly standing when I descended upon her, my hands landing directly on both of her ample breasts! I jumped back as if I'd been shot, as the husband roared something about my questionable ancestry. Thankfully, from a distance Shirley had seen the entire thing unfold but was unable to get through the crowd to help me. Embarrassed and a little shook-up, I apologized profusely, then bought the couple a bottle of white wine to have with dinner. But in my heart, I don't think the guy ever totally believed Shirley or me when we explained my poor vision.

Up to the present, the employees in the places I play tease me that when I make my way down the bar or through the room, I never bump into the burly dudes, it's always a woman. Well think about it. They nearly always smell much better. Another bullet dodged.

31. Snag that Critter!

It's comforting to know I'm not the only one with vision issues that's had an off-the-wall experience, or three. A very low-vision female colleague told me the following embarrassing moment:

She said, "I was attending a new release of a hit movie with a couple girlfriends of mine, and we arrived at the theater just as the show was starting. I couldn't see the screen but loved the experience of being there with my friends. We slid into our row, and I waited for them to tell me which seat I was to take. We were trying to be quiet and not disturb the others around us as we moved in toward the middle. We were nearly at our seats, when I felt something tugging gently on my coat near the front buttons. Assuming I'd caught it on the back of a seat in the row ahead, I gently tugged my coat away, and taking a few more steps, sat down in my seat. My friends did the same, and we settled back to enjoy the show.

When I reached down to open my coat to take it off, I felt a large, furry mass on my lap. I touched it with both hands and screamed loudly, thinking some furry nocturnal varmint that roamed the theater had befriended me. My fingers became entangled in its fur, and still screaming, I jerked my hands away. The thing caught on my ring and flew straight up in the air as if shot from a cannon. As it descended and landed a few rows away, my two friends started laughing hysterically, not capable of explaining to me what had just happened.

I was shaken and confused as my friends helped me sit back down. After I'd calmed down, and they had finally caught their breath, they told me what had occurred. Evidently, as I moved along the seats of the row in front of us, the button on my coat had snagged the wig off a woman sitting in that row. As I tugged on the coat, I'd pulled her wig off, leaving it hanging on my button! After it came free, and I'd thrown it halfway to the ceiling. Without saying a word, the poor, unwillingly shorn woman got up and retrieved it. Promptly, she fled the scene of my innocent shoplift to replace it in the ladies' room.

32. It's all in how you look at it!

My son was growing up, and to my pride and sometimes dismay, he wanted to be a musician. I had started him on drums when he was four, and he really had a gift for percussion. I have always believed to play some instruments at a professional level you have to be born with a great bit of natural ability. Piano, voice, percussion, and pipe organ are a few. If you don't agree, watch a church or pipe organist play sometime. They manipulate two or three manuals or levels of keyboards in front of them, changing stops and pipe settings from the dozens of selectors arranged around them, while playing a two or three octave array of bass pedals with their feet.

Only a few years passed, and my son and his friends were making enough racket in the garage to wake Jimmy Hendrix and Buddy Rich from their repose. One afternoon, I took some time off from teaching to go to his school to watch him play the drum set in a talent show. He won first place, but I discovered later that he cut up one of my custom-tailored silk stage outfits to make a costume for the show! I was listening to the kids, and when the show ended my fifth-grade son came and got me from the audience. He introduced me to some of the teachers and his friends, and as we were walking out of the auditorium, I heard two boys talking behind us as they walked out. The first boy said, "Hey Billy, that's Tony's dad. He plays the guitar and sings in night clubs."

The second boy answered, "Heck, that's no big deal. My Uncle Larry plays the guitar too, and he's in a heavy metal rock band that practices down the street."

Then the first boy continued, "Yeah, Billy, but Tony's dad's blind."

Billy's voice got excited, as he blurted, "Alright! Hey, that's neat!"

33. Easy Come, Easy Go

Janet owned a wonderful restaurant and lounge on the bay at Jack London Square in Oakland, California. The day I auditioned, the manager (with whom my agent had set up the audition) had to talk her into coming across the street from her office to hear me play and sing. She'd heard so many musicians and "friends of friends" audition in the past months that one more warbler was more than she could handle. She told me later that she had crossed the street under duress and had stuck her head into the lounge with the intent of hearing one song. Thank God she liked what she heard, and I started work a month later.

The dance floor of the lounge at the restaurant was in the corner of the building, looking out over the estuary and the beautiful yachts and sailboats anchored around the nearby docks. I played there for three years, my back against the corner in one of the loveliest spots I've ever performed. I played music three nights: Thursday through Saturday, and Sunday brunch. I took pride in my ability to take requests, sing in other languages, and play a wide variety of music styles.

One early summer evening, with the setting sun behind me, I heard someone approaching from the bar. I was in the middle of a request: Jimmy Buffett's old hit "Margaritaville." The lady sounded to be in her forties, and from her speech was well on her way to establishing a magnificent hangover for the next day. "Hey, good looker," she blurted, "why don't you play "Margaritaville?"". With that, she shoved a bill down my open shirt darned near down to my shorts!

A little confused, I waited until the end of a phrase I was singing, and then said, "I'm sorry ma'am, but that's the song I'm singing right now." She was silent for a few seconds, and I heard her move back, listening to me continue with the tune, and then again slurred, "Well, I'll be damned, it is." With that, she bent over me 'til she was almost in my lap and reached down my shirt, retrieved the money and wobbled away.

34. Thanks, Cap'n B.

Try something quite different as you read the following. Pretend you're blindfolded and try to visualize and experience the narrative and descriptive action from the unique perspective of someone who doesn't see.

As we go through our younger life, the adults around us have such a profound effect on our future thinking and actions. If we're very fortunate, at some time in our adult life someone comes along with that same impact. They may change our thinking, help us through a tough period or crisis, or just be a friend. In my life, I was lucky enough to have two men who did all the above.

My brother-in-law Barry was a gifted and successful architect and artist. I was told he weighed over 220, was athletic, and stood six four. He had fine features, with light brown hair and quick moving, intense eyes. Next to his family, he loved most the robust activities of life that gave him escape from the stress of his competitive business. He rarely turned down a chance to have a few brews with the guys at the docks or to drop everything and take off to "crew" on somebody's boat for a weekend race. He loved sailing, fishing— anything remotely connected to the ocean. To him, the ocean was a beautiful and unpredictable woman, and just as challenging. He appreciated a good salty joke, a clever pun, or a well-turned limerick, and had the most cutting wit of any man I've met before or since. He volunteered funds to help get my first business started. It's obvious I admired him and considered him one of my closest friends.

The weather was clear and windy as we pulled up to the parking lot of the yacht club in Barry's Porsche. Looking out over the harbor of Newport Beach, he described the rows of sleek yachts. In irregular lines were motor sailors, smaller cabin cruisers, and pleasure crafts. All were tied along the immaculate piers, slowly rocking as if they were stallions chomping in anticipation of a run across the downs. The well-groomed people walking about seemed to have no singular purpose, not much caring about the activity around them. Most were the epitome of the image of California's "beautiful people." Hundreds milled about with a quiet, almost enviable illusion and aura of success.

Barry said some of the yachts were breathtaking; a few were over a hundred feet in length, and many were in the fifty to seventy-five-foot range. I'm sure the average person wouldn't have the means to pay the docking fees on some of the cruisers, not to mention the insurance, upkeep, and exorbitant fuel cost. Barry said it would take nearly two grand to fill the fuel tanks of some of the larger ones. I remember thinking, "That's a big chunk of change for some leisure time frolicking on the Pacific." Professionals, doctors, corporate heads, and movie moguls owned the majority of these boats.

As we made our way along the piers, Barry described some of the tourist attractions. He named off the restaurants, smaller eateries, and one particular clam and lobster house whose bar we'd frequent and close much later that night. Occasionally, there'd be a lilt of appreciation in his voice as he watched and described a full-figured, bronzed and beautiful woman pass by. I remarked, "The worst damn drawback about losing my sight is not being able to look at beautiful women anymore."

He replied, "Hell, Bubba, maybe if you keep playing that guitar and are persuasive enough, they just might let you check them out in Braille." It was a threadbare quip, but I laughed anyway.

I remember the air had a certain smell, a different scent than the harbors and wharves mooring working boats. Missing was the smell of decaying fish, old oxidized marine paint, burned diesel oil, and the pungent odor of plankton-coated nets drying in the sun. I was surprised at the absence of shrieks and cries of the hundreds of gulls normally circling and swooping for food around the working wharves. Here at Newport the air was a fascinating mixture of grilling hamburgers and pickle relish, gasoline fumes, expensive perfume and after-shave, tanning oil, and deodorized perspiration. And I swear as we passed by one large motor cruiser, I noticed the unmistakable perfume-like aroma of newly shaken gin martinis float by my nose.

I was gently holding Barry's left elbow, and since I wasn't using my cane, we moved briskly along the pier. Occasionally, he'd warn me to step over a vagrant rope, cable, or piece of equipment on the heavy planks. Soon near the end of the docks we found his sailboat, the *Sea Song*, a forty-foot fiberglass hulled masterpiece. She was thirty years old, and Barry said he'd completely refurbished all of her exterior and interior wood. He'd also rebuilt or replaced practically every moving mechanical part on the boat. She was true labor of love.

After a few minutes removing the canvas weather cover from the cockpit, he helped me over the gunwale and onto the cushioned seats. I sat down facing the bow as he immediately began storing the gear we'd brought on board. Included were sandwiches, beer, sunscreen, and a half-filled thermos of brandied coffee, its contents partially sacrificed earlier that morning. I heard Barry leap from the cockpit and onto the decking above the cabin, as the boat slightly moved from the weight of his large frame. Yet, I could hear he moved with the agility of a big cat. He set to work removing the sails and rigging from the forward sail locker near the bow. As he worked, my curious fingers explored the wonders of the *Sea Song's* control panel. I felt the smooth, warm metal of the helm. It was circular, made of chrome or stainless steel, and a single small handle jutted out toward the stern. From all my childhood readings, I'd expected a wooden wheel with spoke handles jutting out all around it. Tracing my fingers across what were probably gauges for the engine, I quickly found the throttle and a row of toggle switches. There was a padded folding seat attached to the starboard bulkhead so the boat could be steered from either a standing or sitting position.

As Barry worked his way aft, I heard his deck shoes squeak as he jumped down into the cockpit and stood at the helm. He flipped a switch, and instantly I heard the whirring sound of the bilge fan. Barry told me hundreds of sailors around the world had met their maker by not completing this procedure. There probably isn't a large harbor on the West Coast of North America that hadn't, at one time or another, had a cruiser blown completely out of the water from exploding bilge gases detonated by an impatient hand on an ignition switch. Ironically, a few years later while I played at Jack London Square on the Bay, the very same fate nailed a yacht owner. Luckily only a second after firing up the engine, he'd jumped onto the dock to go pay a fuel bill at the pump dock a few yards away. This saved his life.

While the fan whirred, Barry showed me the two fire extinguishers on deck and how they operated, as well as the location of the first aid kit below the control console. He turned and ducked into the cabin. I heard the unmistakable sound of a hand-turned cork. Seconds later he emerged, handing me a plastic cup containing an ample portion of Hennessy Cognac. "Only one sip for me," he said as we toasted to women, boats, and music. Barry then exclaimed, "Hell, Ahab, let's invade Catalina and rape and pillage! How are you at pillaging?" He manipulated a few more lines, then opened a rear compartment and took out some life preservers. Handing me one he said, "You won't like this, but put it on anyway. I don't know how bombed you're going to get, and I wouldn't want you falling ass-over-haircut into the Pacific Ocean." In two long steps he crossed the cabin, reached inside and flipped another switch, and I heard the crackling of a ship-to-shore short wave radio. Instantly it announced weather reports, and as Barry moved the dial, we heard the chatter of party fishing boats swapping information about the location of fish. Skippers were asking for Coast Guard information, inquiring about tides and wind velocities.

I heard the whir of the starter as the engine turned over and came to life, its exhaust bubbling and gurgling beneath the stern. Barry said proudly, "Doesn't that baby sound sweet? I just had her completely rebuilt, new bearings, valves, push rods, and everything. Man, that pile of junk that was in here before made such a damned racket, she sounded like a Russian submarine. I was embarrassed to take her out." He hopped up, moving forward, untied the line from the dock, and secured it forward. In only seconds he was back by my side at the helm. Barry handled the *Sea Song* like she was an eight-foot dinghy. A masterful sailor, his skill was well known around the harbor. He dropped the engine into reverse and cracked the throttle, giving it a few revs, pulling the stern away from the dock. Then shifting to forward gear, we moved slowly down the slip toward the opening of the channel.

As we slid quietly along in the calm water, we passed some of the big motor cruisers. Some were literally floating palaces. On one, Barry said though it was still two and a half hours till lunch, they were having one hell of a bash. A five-piece jazz band was playing on the fantail, complete with sax, electric guitar, and full drums. About thirty people were strolling around the decks with cocktails. Many were laughing, oblivious to the rest of the world. He said, "Ahab, I wish you could see the lamps on that brunette!"

Grinning, I said, "Shut up, man, you're a cruel dude!" I could feel the solid vibration of the steady engine as the Sea Song moved forward through the small swell. She had a feeling of solid seaworthiness about her. As we passed the breakwater, Barry opened her to full throttle, and we picked up speed. I felt a change in the length of the swells and knew we were now in the open ocean. We changed course to north/northwest, and Barry told me to take the wheel. "You sure?"

"Hell yes, Bubba," he laughed, "I'm goin' to work your ass off today." He climbed forward and yelled, "We're clear on this course, there's nothing ahead, so hold her at this heading while I run up some sail. I'll give you a holler if we fall off course." Lord! I was holding the helm like I was hanging from the ledge of a ten-story building. I was excited but had a knot in the pit of my gut as big as a softball. Man, what if I screw up and accidentally hit something on this panel, or ram this beautiful baby into something?

The light-headedness from my few sips of Hennessy had quickly disappeared as the excitement increased my heart rate. I heard Barry moving forward again and heard the thump of a hatch cover as he descended into the forward sail locker. Soon the rustling of nylon and Dacron came from forward, then the snapping of metal shackles as he set to work at the bow. I noticed an undulation in the engine RPM's as the prow would clear each swell and slide down into the trough in between each wave crest. It seemed Barry had only been forward for a few minutes when I felt a complete change in the pitch of the deck and the tension of the rudder as he ran up the jib. The stern lifted as the bow dug deeper into the swells ahead. Then Barry made his way aft, half-singing and whistling. He loved music, but man, he couldn't sing a lick!

On the cabin top he began uncoiling lines at the base of the mainmast. I heard the whirring of a wench. Then it dawned on me why he'd earlier removed the sail cover from the main mast boom. The big sail began ascending as the wind grabbed and snapped it, popping the edges of the material loudly. In only a moment the sleek craft was transformed into a stallion's leaping, frolicking colt, just released for the first time into the wide-open pasture. Whoa, baby! For a second, I couldn't handle the helm! The water pressure against the rudder was totally different under sail. I felt like a locomotive engineer on a runaway freight train. Barry gave out a big belly laugh and again jumped into the cockpit. I released my death grasp on the helm as he took it and killed the engine.

Sliding my hands down the teak railing of the cockpit, I found a seat. He changed headings, cramping the sails into the wind as she heeled over to starboard. The wind took hold, and then we were soaring, a feeling I'll never forget. I'd sailed before, but only on small lake sailors and sailing dinghies, carrying the weight of someone with me, slowing the little boats down. This was the most exhilarating feeling I'd ever experienced.

The strong wind pressing against the sails caused the main mast to vibrate and shudder, sending a low-frequency vibration throughout the hull. I could feel the strength and resiliency of the hull as it bent and gave to the onslaughts of the rolling swells before us. She leapt and challenged each new wave. Barry told me to take over the helm again. I braced against the starboard gunwale. It was difficult to stand, for now, she'd canted-over many degrees. Barry explained, "You hold her on this heading. Occasionally you'll need to crank her a bit to port, 'cause she'll drift off to starboard from the force of the wind." In only seconds I knew what he meant, for the strong wind pushed the angle of the bow, and she'd fall off readily. I had to correct it by counter steering in the opposite direction. The sound of the luffing and slapping of the sails warned me instantly when I wasn't steering at the proper wind angle. Barry yelled words of encouragement every so often, saying the sea ahead was clear. I completely lost track of time. Nothing seemed to be more important except that moment, where I was, what I was doing, and the pure joy of the experience. My hair, beard, and upper half of me were soaked. I felt a simple kinship with those sailors from centuries before. Maybe I was feeling that same emotion of freedom, respect, and fear, unique to rock and mountain climbing, flying, or challenging the depths of the sea.

After about an hour, Barry took the helm again, and I asked if it was okay to go forward to the bow. He said all right, but insisted I take a short piece of cable with two snap shackles and use it as a tether. We clipped one end to my belt and the other to the strong cable running around the edge of the deck, from midship to the bow. He laughed saying, "This way if you fall on your ass and go overboard, you'll just hang there like a smoked salmon until I can get up there to reel you in." Because of his marvelous humor I never felt foolish around him. Slowly working my way forward toward the bow, every few feet I'd release the snap shackle from the cable. Then skipping over the stanchion going down to the deck, I connected it to the next section of cable. When I finally reached the point of the prow, I was able to stand with my feet wide apart grasping the chrome railing jutting out over the bow. God, what a thrill!

This area of the boat, as best as I can describe it, was somewhat like the approach to a diving board only instead the bars made a U-shaped loop out over the prow. Many times, in rougher seas, the structure would be totally submerged as the bow plowed into high waves. Today, however, the swells were wide and of medium height, so the bow was never submerged. I felt a slight cavitation from left to right as the yacht knifed through the water with a tremendous rise and fall at the prow and stern, as she climbed and descended each moving swell. It was like a seagoing roller coaster. I can truthfully say, outside of making love, I can't think of many other experiences more euphoric or exhilarating.

The sounds around me assaulted my ears: the thunderous slap of the *Sea Song's* bow as she crashed into each oncoming wave, the whooshing of the sea splitting by the bow, breaking into spray, bathing everything behind with salty mist. Accompanying these sensations were the sounds of the wind whistling in my ears and nostrils and the high-pitched singing of the topside wire cables of the main mast. This symphony of ocean sounds was assaulted by Barry's off-pitch baritone attempting a raucous limerick, "There once was a sailor named Ben, who one night drank far too much gin. Climbing up to his ship, on a beer can he slipped, and never was heard from again."

There was something simplistic, yet timeless about what I was experiencing this day. It reminded me of the hundreds of books about the sea I'd read as a teenager. Suddenly, it was the middle 1800's, and I was at the giant wheel of a tall square-rigger rounding Cape Horn. Or maybe I was Captain Hornblower commanding the Lydia, or perhaps Sir Francis Drake on the Golden Hind, heading off to new discoveries in the South Seas. I was brought back to reality by Barry yelling, "Hang on, Ahab, we're coming about." He cranked the helm to port and we immediately fell off beneath the wind, the stern turning slowly away from the source of our power. The boat slowly slid to a stop, wallowing gently in the swells, her limp sails slapping in the brisk wind. Barry loosened the metal cables going to the tip of the mast, sliding the mainsail and jib down toward the boom. We began drifting in the intense sun. Barry said, "Time out, Bubba. The chow lamp is lit, let's have some lunch."

We pulled off our shirts and lay back against the side of the cockpit, our feet on the railing, letting the wind blow around us. We made a frontal assault on a pile of deli ham and cheese sandwiches, soft pretzels with mustard, and cold beer, and then polished off the feast with some fresh cherry turnovers Barry had picked up at the bakery that morning. We talked a long time, and he related some things I'm sure he'd never told anyone before. Personal thoughts, some of the facets of his life he enjoyed, and a few others bugging him big-time. His most troubling concern was the toll the rising stress his successful architectural business was taking on his mind and marriage.

Suddenly, our conversation was interrupted by a strange and fascinating sound. Barry said, "Approaching off to starboard about a hundred yards is a pod of four gray whales. Might be a male in front; he's damn near twice the size of the others behind, although in some whale species the female is larger." In a moment I heard them pass by so close, I swear I could smell their breath and the kelpy scent of their bodies. They slid by, blowing and making a marvelous hissing, shushing sound from their blowholes. I remembered the time at the old Klamath Theater as a kid when I saw the movie, "Moby Dick". I recalled how sick to my stomach I became after watching those gigantic animals being slaughtered by the whalers, and it disgusts me to this day to think some of these wonderful creatures are still being hunted.

Barry said the bright sun had been more intense than usual, soon convincing us to put our shirts back on. I grabbed my Giants cap from the gear bag we'd brought on board. Rummaging for the sunscreen, I heard Barry switch on the radio, and I listened, trying to make out the latest weather report. He said, "There's a front rollin' down from Monterey. The wind will pick up soon. It's time to haul this girl around and head south." At that moment a mixture of real emotions swept over me. There on the sea there was so much tranquility and simplicity. I wanted to stay out there for a week.

Barry climbed up to the cabin top and reset the sails. In only moments, we were close-hauled and on our way. He said not to worry about the heading; he'd help me with it as soon as he got the sails fine trimmed. Barry took the helm again, and as he changed headings, I slid down the padded seats and kicked back with my feet on the railing. I found and sipped on the remainder of my warm cognac I'd managed to nurse for the past few hours. After the couple of beers with lunch, I was grateful I'd taken the Dramamine the day before and earlier that morning. If I hadn't, by now, my grill wouldn't have been a palatable sight after we'd wallowed in the swell, dead in the water for an hour.

We were soon heading downwind on a southeasterly tack with the wind off our starboard stern. "She's all yours again, Ahab, just keep her keel down, that's all I ask," Barry said, his voice smiling. I heard Barry humming something I couldn't recognize as he swung the main boom out to port to catch the wind. With it behind us, it felt as if we were moving smoother through the water, yet we were sailing faster. It seemed like such a short time, but hours had passed. I felt the sun getting lower as it warmed my back. As he took the helm again, Barry said we were approaching the mainland. I moved forward and ducked inside the cabin. After a visit to the head, I found my battered shoulder bag, and packed and lit my old French bulldog pipe. At the moment, I was feeling very much like an "old salt". Barry yelled at me, calling me that name further solidifying my "old Saltness." "Ahab, I sure as hell wish you could see this, it's quite a sight." I moved back out of the cabin and sat as he described the scene before him. "She was an old ocean liner, evidently built in Denmark, was owned by the Norwegians, and as the story goes was sold to some South American country."

Confused, I asked, "Where is she?"

Like an old sea captain, he ignored me and continued, engrossed in his story. "They used it as a cruise ship for some years. I heard she foundered on the beach here during a hell of a storm back in the early fifties. She looks about four or five hundred feet in length, a pretty good size, may have had two main screws. She's lying on her starboard side. Some time or another, she'd been burned. The damn awesome thing about it is, she's lying on the sand way up there. It must be a good three hundred yards from the shoreline." I heard him unsnap his binoculars to further inspect the wreck. "Man, somebody spent an awful long time cannibalizing her. All the portholes are gone. There's probably not a piece of brass or copper left in her. From this angle I can't see the screws, but it looks like the rudder's gone."

I tried to visualize what he was seeing, and it brought home the realization of the power and force of the sea. Sometime in the past, the crashing sea had thrown this huge vessel on the shore like an angry child discarding a broken toy. Barry changed the heading a few degrees and we continued south toward Newport Beach. The wind suddenly increased and under its force, the boat heeled even further over to port. We picked up a few more knots and was fairly tearing through the water, dancing and bouncing as if on a sea-borne sleigh ride. Being tight hauled now, she healed very far, the port gunwale was nearly flush with the surface of the water. We hooked our elbows over the teak railing, bracing ourselves with our feet nearly dangling below us. We soon were laughing and singing, giving Jack London a run for his grog, "We're sailing 'cross the river from Liverpool; heave away Santiano, 'round Cape Horn to 'Frisco Bay, way out in Californio."

Continuing south, we'd ran out of sandwiches, and sadly the pretzels were history. Suddenly I was struck with the reason why most sailors do most of their imbibing while ashore. I knew my face must've been turning green by degrees, certainly not in visual harmony with the blue of the Pacific. At that point, I started planning the most direct route to the railing downwind, in case the tortured contents of my stomach decided not to stay at their present address. Luckily, the nausea passed.

The warmth of the sun was gone. It was near sunset, and as if on cue, the wind slackened, smoothing out the ground swells. Barry flicked a switch on the control panel, and below, a small generator came to life. He said he was switching on the running lights and explained, "That pup below works hard. We wouldn't be able to keep the lights, depth finder, and radio going for long just running on the batteries." Barry was conscientious, and always bought top-notch equipment, making sure everyone on board knew how to use it. He always studied the latest charts and kept up on all the rules and regulations of the Coast Guard.

The closer we got to the coast, the colder it seemed to get. The wind continued to slacken, and we kept her under full sail. I'd take the helm alternately with Barry while he watched the shoreline for familiar landmarks and buoy markers. Occasionally, he'd flip on the radio to check the weather and listen for any changes out of the ordinary. There were few sounds in the night air, only an occasional helicopter or airplane passing in the distance, the far-off lonesome clanging of a bell buoy, and the ever-present slapping of waves at the bow.

Barry yelled back at me, " Bubba, you're doing fine. Keep her on this same heading. I'm goin' forward to knock down the jib. We've got a ways to go before we get to the harbor entrance. Just hang tight. I'll come back and start the engine in a few minutes." He clambered forward, and I heard the jib fall and recognized the familiar snap of the clips as he took each one from the jib as it fell. He came aft and repeated the same with the mainsail. We instantly lost headway as the boat slowed to a near stop. After blowing the bilge fumes, Barry again started the engine and said, "I set her at half-throttle, so she'll be easy. You might have to swing her starboard or port a few degrees. I'll give you a yell if we have to make a big change." I did what he said, not having a clue what was in front of us. Barry ran along the main boom, fastening the furled main sail, quickly attaching each sail clamp while singing softly under his breath: "It's only me from over the sea, said Barnacle Bill the sailor. I'm old and rough and dirty and tough, said Barnacle Bill the sailor."

He yelled, "Ease back on the throttle a little bit, Ahab, we want to drop some RPM's. We're coming up on the main buoy. I have to stow some lines and lock something's down." I asked him how the heading was, and he replied, "You're doing great for now, just keep her straight ahead." The boat was so much different under engine power. Only a few minutes before, she was a floating ballerina. But now she felt like dancing with a gal who couldn't follow your lead. Every movement took effort. Her controls seemed sloppy, and I felt a definite time lapse between the helm and the water pressure on the rudder.

"Hey Barry, don't you think you better take over?"

"Nah man, not yet," he bellowed, "she's still yours for a while, give her a little bend to starboard."

Ten minutes later, with his directions we were plying slowly through the harbor entrance. I'd be a liar if I said I wasn't scared stupid. I'm sure the white knuckles were back. All afternoon on the open ocean I'd felt so free and comfortable with the beautiful boat, but at that moment, I felt so vulnerable and a little paranoid knowing there were things ahead I couldn't see. I yelled out, "Barry, hey Barry! I'm sorry man, but I feel as worthless as a screen door in a submarine right now. Be sure and let me know if I have to change the heading."

He yelled back, "A little to port and back the throttle." I did what he asked and heard him again. "Great, we're lookin' good, just give me a minute."

I heard the clanging of bell buoys and the slapping of cables against aluminum masts in the distance. Muffled voices and music seemed to be coming from one of the yachts off to port. I knew how sound travels at night, so things weren't as close as they seemed, but in the cool night air, I thought my ears were playing tricks on me. "Everything alright ahead?" I croaked. Barry yelled from the bow sail locker, his voice strong and reassuring, "Hey Bubba, you're handling this baby like Admiral Nelson, so relax. Don't worry, you're doing great! Things are still open around us. Crank her a half turn to starboard, and I'll be back there soon. I've got a couple of fouled lines up here."

We kept idling along, the nearly silent engine pushing us slowly through the water. I kept listening, cocking my head trying to hear better, then would hold my breath and listen again. Finally, I couldn't take it anymore. I yelled, "Hey, Barry! Barry! Damn it, how are we doing on the heading?"

Instantly I heard the thump of his feet on the steps of the front sail locker and then heard words that will forever be indelibly chiseled in my memory. As he scrambled aft, he bellowed, "OH, CHRIST! STARBOARD ROY, DAMN IT! HARD STARBOARD FAST!"

At that instant, I didn't know which way to turn the helm! Suddenly, after all the books I'd read and all the times I'd been on boats, I couldn't remember port from starboard. At that moment, I didn't know my own name. Adrenaline shot through me like an electric shock. I guess instinctively, as if some guiding force was moving my hands, I spun the wheel rapidly to the right. The great God of sailboats, blind guys and absent-minded skippers was watching over us that evening. I felt the *Sea Song's* bow move slowly then quicker to starboard. Then, he was standing next to me mumbling half under his breath, "Dear, sweet Lord, that was too close." He took the helm, slapping me on the back as he said, "Good job, Ahab. My fault. I started thinking about a contract bid that's due this week. We just missed an anchored eighty-foot schooner by about twenty feet!"

We idled slowly on into the slip. In just a few minutes we were alongside the pier. Barry grabbed a gnarly rope from the dock and handed it to me, then worked his way forward to tie down. I hung onto the rope as if it was holding me, dangling over the Grand Canyon, tying me to the solid safety of the earth. I wondered how we made it into the harbor under my expert guidance. Barry jumped on the dock and walked toward me. I handed him the canvas bag containing the shrapnel from our day's groceries. He effortlessly helped me up onto the dock, and with a grin in his voice roared, "Well Ahab, this last leg of the ride leaves me with only one thing to say: Let's have a drink or four!"

The last I remember of that day was sitting on the little stage in the bar of Willie's Wharf, my belly full of oysters, garlic bread and steamed clams, with somebody's beat-up twelve-string guitar in my lap. I was amazed at the line of free drinks off to my side. Secretly I'd wished the kind folks would've given me cash in lieu of liquid offerings, but, "Oh well." I was strumming with reckless abandon, singing loudly those same timeless, ribald seafarers songs Barry dearly loved, while the bar crowd clapped and sang along. The more off-color the song, the louder they sang, "There once was a sailor named Bates, who could do the fandango on skates. But he tripped on his cutlass, which rendered him nut-less and practically worthless on dates!"

Looking back now to that marvelous day, I can say it was a unique and unforgettable experience. As we said decades ago at Disneyland, "That was an E-ticket ride!" I'm sure it was something I'll never experience again, and I know now why Barry let me stay at the helm for those priceless hours. On that windy day I was Errol Flynn, or Captain Cook, or maybe just another sailor feeling the magic of the sea. Barry's retired now, spending a lot of time in Guam. He's still enjoying frequent dates with his first love, the Pacific. He will always have my thanks for the memory of his special gift to me, that priceless day on the ocean off Newport Beach.

35. Fork in The Road

As the years and months passed, despite some gut-wrenching trials, I continued to play regularly and teach. There are so many wonderful stories and tales of people and situations that I could fill two more volumes. Still, the most gratifying thing to me is teaching. There is no greater high than watching a student succeed and grow and knowing you had input in the process.

While teaching for the federal CETA program, I visited a very magical site in Fremont Ca.: the newly moved California School for the Blind (C.S.B.). The superintendent took me on a tour of the soon to be opened campus. When we were finished, we stood in the center of the "Town Square" of the new residential school. A strange feeling came over me. There was something very compelling and mysterious about what I was experiencing at that moment. I knew that day that I would someday be a part of this magical place.

From the first day I taught my first class there, I understood what a special place it is. I like to think of it as a sanctuary, an educational mixing bowl, and a launching pad for some very special students. You can still walk into any of my large classes and hear me greet my students with a raucous "Hello, lovely people!" I've taught there for over three decades and still can hardly wait to get to work each morning— sure beats cleaning out storm drains!

The following scenes have been included in this book for their humor and entertainment value. They show some of the remarkable attributes of some of our special students and should never in any way be construed as exploitative or demeaning to their disability. Remember, for every one of the bizarre or humorous situations that follow, there are a dozen others as common and downright brilliant as your own child's daily achievements.

36. Here's the Kicker

People often ask me, since I can't see, how I know so much about the way my students look. That's easy, because I love to visualize. I always have my wife, fellow teachers, or teaching assistants describe the general physical characteristics of my students: height, hair color, and general build, etc. It helps me feel as though I am approaching them more as a sighted person, but certainly doesn't give me any preconceived ideas of what they can or can't do.

I had only taught at CSB for a few weeks when I found I could throw everything I'd ever been taught about traditional teaching techniques out the window. I'd taught for years, but strangely, never taught a visually impaired child before coming to the school. The first day of my primary music activity class, I'd carefully set out all the hand percussion instruments and materials I'd need for that day. My acoustic guitar was tuned and ready, and my mind was filled with every diddle-diddle, pop-pop song I knew. Mr. Rogers, you've moved over, now let me boogie! As the students came in, the room was soon filled with a mixture of crying, laughing, sleeping "hyper" blind children, making enough noise to wake Louis Braille from the grave.

One particular young fellow, we'll call him Sammy, was soon entertaining himself by clearing everything from the tables with the sweeping motions of his hummingbird-like arms. His harried and distraught teacher had her hands full with the five other kids in her class, but Sammy was as uncapturable as a good literary agent. He slid under chairs, tables, pianos, and various and sundry other pieces of classroom equipment. After he'd finished wiping out most of the things on my desk in one swell foop, I suddenly became a man with a purpose.

What I didn't know then was that Sammy had a great deal of vision and was most adept at using it to his clandestine advantage. I finally captured one of his ankles as he hid under the grand piano in the corner of the room. He'd hooked his legs around the damper pedals, hanging on for dear life, something I remember doing quite similarly somewhere in my distant childhood. On my hands and knees under the piano, I was finally able to pry him loose and unceremoniously placed him in one of the chairs in the front row. His teacher thanked me profusely and told him to sit still and not leave the chair under penalty of no snack before recess. I turned, adjusted my tie, and was heading back to my teaching station, somewhat ruffled and taken down a few rungs off the professional teacher's demeanor ladder, when I heard quick steps behind me. Instantly I felt a searing pain in the back of my leg as Sammy delivered a solid kick behind my knee. Believe me, Sammy could have made it as a striker on any World Cup soccer team. I'm sure my mouth dropped open as Sammy sailed by my left side in a straight line to my guitar. The race was on! I caught him just as the strings were twanging from his grabbing at the instrument. I managed to get a hold on the back of his jeans, taking the guitar away.
I know this was probably an excellent opportunity for a meaningful teaching experience, endowing the young man with useful information concerning the values of not touching others' property without first asking their permission, but for some reason, the moment succumbed to other needs.

Suddenly, I felt like a fisherman off Baja who'd just hooked his first Marlin, and I was determined to bring it aboard. Sammy had no intention of being landed, stuffed, or taken to his seat. I think looking back now, I won two out of three falls, but Sammy gave me some anxious moments. Finally getting him back in his seat with the help of the teacher's assistant, I thundered in my best operatic voice for him to remain there, or he'd be eaten by a vicious troll (or something similar). I guess the big voice helped, for to my surprise, he stayed in his seat for the rest of the class!

Now I'll cop to it, his behavior improved markedly when I promised him if he'd stay put in future classes, at the end of the period, he could sit behind the drum set and hit the sticks on the cymbals. Later in the year, he actually helped me put away instruments at the end of class, another triumph for sugar over vinegar. It's quite possible they were kidding, but the next year, someone said Sammy's teacher had left the school and was counting penguins at Ross Island for the Audubon Society in Antarctica.

I soon met a student who would be with me for nearly ten years. My first lesson on the piano with Becky, she informed me the damned piano was out of tune, and she wasn't going to play it until it was. She promptly flopped down on the floor and took off both shoes. Making use of her minimal vision, she then proceeded to throw them across the room at the window. Ironically, she was correct. The instrument was a little off, and I had it tuned the next week. Becky was one of those marvelous kids who have a gift. She was a true savant. Anything she heard, she played, often after only hearing the piece once. She amazed me nearly every day. Tall and thin, she wasn't able to carry on a simple conversation, except about things she was interested in or impressed with at the moment, i.e. food, music, TV, etc. Becky could imitate voices and singers' vocal styles with uncanny accuracy. She would play the piano and accompany herself, sounding one minute like Barbra Streisand and then moments later like Natalie Cole or Ray Charles. Some recording artists released the song, "We Are the World," as a fundraiser for world hunger, and Becky immediately learned it, imitating every artist on the record. She performed it in one of our concerts at C.S.B. and was the hit of the night. She had over a three -octave range and memorized lyrics amazingly fast. The only negative was, she usually didn't have a clue what the words meant. But Becky was something very special. Her only other pastime besides playing and singing music was eating soda crackers and listening and memorizing the dialogue of soap operas and TV sit-coms.

One afternoon near the holiday season, I'd taken our small jazz ensemble into the theater to practice for the coming concert. Becky was of course the lead vocalist and keyboard player. Our microphones were on, and we were working hard when the superintendent of our school came in with some important visitors from the Special Education Office in Sacramento. "Okay if we listen for a minute, Mr. Oliver?" she said as we finished a song we were working on.

"Sure," I said, "come on up to the stage." I had just turned to the drummer and was telling him the tune we were going to rehearse, when I heard Becky's heavy breathing through her mic. I should have expected what was about to happen, for often with no reason, Becky would repeat lines she'd heard on TV or the radio.

I was puzzled and about to ask what was wrong, when she spoke over the mike in a low, sexy voice, "OH, Mr. Oliver" (there was a long pause as she breathed in with a low, sultry hiss), "but Mr. Oliver, you don't...you don't give me all your love."

I clearly heard a gasp from one of our visitors as a cold chill came over me. I saw my job and reputation exiting the premises as I tried to come up with some kind of coherent reply. Then I blurted, "No, not right now Becky. I know how much you like that song, but it's not really appropriate for here at school, maybe you can do it later, just for yourself."

Both the students and staff had a collection of "Becky-isms" to share over the years. Often when it was raining, she'd come in from outside soaking wet, for she refused to wear a rain hat or use an umbrella. She'd feel the dripping water coming from her drenched hair and exclaim, "My hair is crying!"

Almost every holiday for many years now, our Jazz Ensemble has had the honor of playing for the State Department of Education's annual holiday party in Sacramento, about a two and a half-hour drive from our school. I remember two wonderful Becky-isms from one of these trips. As we entered the city, we passed a construction site where workmen were using a jackhammer to break up concrete. Becky announced loudly, "Please, Mr. Oliver, make them stop fighting that war!"

The band was dressed in black vests and pants, with white shirts and blouses for the gig. We climbed out of the van and Becky looked down at her outfit, announcing loudly, "Well, now I'm a police car!"

Her favorite expression when confused or not understanding what was going on around her was, "My brain is sick."

37. Tell it Like it is

At C.S.B., we receive many wonderful donations and tools for our students. One year, the phone company loaned us some unique and useful telephone demonstrators. They were very expensive pieces of equipment, built in a way so the teacher could sit across from the student, with a wall in between, holding phones on either side. They were electrically operated with dial tones and amplified voices when either the student or teacher spoke into their phone. As I remember, we were loaned two of the units to teach the kids to use 911 and the push-button dial feature. As it goes sometimes, we didn't start the students on the trainers right away, for it was the beginning of the year, and other scheduling concerns were more important at the time. A few weeks later, a spokesman from the company called and said he was bringing out some executives from their headquarters to videotape our kids in action with the new trainers. We immediately went into high gear, trying to give a couple of students a crash course in how to use the equipment. April, fourteen years old, was a particularly good candidate for the task, for she had a wonderful gift for memorizing instructions and reciting back anything she'd been prompted to say.

Later in the week, smiling, the folks from the phone company arrived and greeted her. The machine was turned on with the principal and other concerned administrators nervously gathered around to see the demonstration of April's newfound skills. With the video camera rolling, her classroom teacher sat across from her on the other side of the trainer and explained the task to April as she waited patiently. "Alright April. You're alone in your house watching television, and you want a glass of milk. As you go into the kitchen, because of your useable vision, you see the stove is on fire with big flames! It's very important for you to do something right away. What do you do?"

"I go to the phone and dial 911," April said in her laconic, almost computer-like voice.

"That's wonderful," the teacher said. "You do that right now, and I'll be the 911 operator." April promptly dialed 911, and as her phone rang loudly, the teacher answered on the other phone.

"Hello, this is the 911 emergency operator. What do you want?"

There was stone silence for a few seconds, then April answered sweetly, "I want a glass of milk"!

38. Go in the Back Door

A few years after I began teaching at C.S.B., I met another great personality. Randy was an overweight, muscular boy with a great happy-go-lucky attitude. He soon after he arrived at the school, he developed a great love for coca-cola and spent every quarter he could get his hands on feeding the two machines on campus. He was told not to, but the lure of sugar and buzz of caffeine was too much. He soon was borrowing money from many of his friends, and even a few enemies through clandestine means. The problem soon surfaced that Randy was rapidly building up a student body debt that would soon rival the loans of a small third world country. The administration then decided he was not to use the machines anymore, and no one including staff was to loan him money under any circumstance. One afternoon after school, I was working in my room when Randy appeared at my open classroom door. "Hello Mr. Oliver," he said in his normal affable tone. "How's it goin'?"

"Just great Randy, what can I do for you?"

"Well Mr. O, I had to go to the work site this afternoon, and the drinking fountain was busted. I ain't had a drink of anything since right after lunch."

"That's a shame, Randy," I said, sounding concerned. "Go on down the hall and let the fountain run for a while and drink all the water you want."

"Ah naw, Mr. O, I was hopin' you'd lend me fifty cents so I could buy me a coke over at the Rec Center."

"Randy," I said firmly, "all of us teachers have been told not to loan or give you money for cokes 'cause the sugar's not good for you, and you owe too many people money."

125

"Oh, I'll pay ya back. I promise," he pleaded.

"No, sorry Randy, I have to stick to the rules just like everybody else. You get on over to the dorms, they'll be looking for you soon." He said nothing and left the music building. Just ten minutes later, he was back at my door.

"Mr. O, I'm sorry to bug ya again, but I got myself in a spot. I need some help." He cleared his throat for a second, then continued. "Ya see, I'm broke, and today's my friend's birthday. And…and, I need to borrow fifty cents. I need fifty cents to buy him a coke for his birthday."

As the months passed, the cokes and second grazings in the dining hall gradually took their toll on the big fella's ample frame, but Randy was always willing and eager to come to music, and he loved to play rhythm instruments and sing. One day during my teen music activity class, some administrators visited me from a local school district. Included in the group was my new boss, the just hired new principal of our school. In no time, I had the class singing and making a joyful noise. Then I noticed Randy wasn't singing or playing his tambourine. That's when I made my first mistake. Singling him out I said, "Randy, you're not singing. Come on, Tiger, we need that fine voice." He said nothing as we plowed on into the next song. At the end of it, I realized he was still not singing, so naturally I decided to stick the needle deeper into my palm. "Come on, Big Guy, we need to hear that tambourine to help us keep on the beat, and we want to hear some singing."

"I can't sing," was his guttural reply. I felt the hair on the back of my neck tingle from the stares of the visitors, eager to see how I'd handle this logjam.

"Sure, you can Randy. You've one of the best voices in the school," I pleaded.

"I can't sing," he repeated firmly. The other students were getting impatient, and I felt like crawling under my chair to make an attempt at removing from my person the dagger I'd chosen to fall on.

"Randy, you always sing with us. What's wrong today? Why can't you sing?"

A pause followed, then he blurted out, "I just can't sing Mr. O. I can't sing 'cause my underwear's too tight."

39. Well, that's what you said, Teach!

Blind children are notorious for being very verbal, but they often don't have a clue as to what the words or phrases they are using actually mean or describe (i.e. singing songs with lyrics perfectly memorized, and yet not knowing or understanding what thoughts or events the words are describing). Years ago, I played the guitar and sang the old English folk song, "The Fox", to a visiting class of bright middle school blind students. I was trying to demonstrate "anthropomorphism," the use of humanlike attributes given to cartoon or fictional animals. I told the students I would be asking them some questions about the song when we were finished. The first line of the song is written:

"The fox went out on a chilly night, he prayed for the moon to give him light, for he'd
many a mile to go that night, before he reached the town-o, town-o, town-o.... etc."
After I'd sung the entire song, I asked the class what it was about. A young lady in the back row answered, "It's about a fox that went into a town."

"That's great," I said, "and what was he doing there?"

Quite seriously, a young man in the front row answered, "He went into town to get some chili!"

Of course, there is always an exception to any broad statement, and some of my students could slither about the English language with reckless abandon, knowing exactly what they were saying, perfectly understanding the situation generating their words. The following is a good example.

For a few years, I taught jazz and rock keyboard to a slight, quite frail teenager who was blessed with a good deal of useable vision. He wore a back brace and thick glasses, and I was told his hair was already graying though he was only fourteen. Nathan was outspoken and opinionated, and not in the least bashful about letting anyone nearby know his viewpoint. He was one of the first students at C.S.B. to have his own computer with large print on the screen, and he spent many hours working with it in his room. Walter, one of the dormitory counselors, told me the following one day at lunch.

One evening after dinner, Walter was leading a group of Boy Scouts over to the theater for their weekly scout meeting. Seeing Nathan alone in his room as always, Walter asked him, "Hey Nathan, why don't you join us and come on over to the scout meeting?"

Walt said Nathan didn't hesitate a second as he looked up and blurted out in indignation, "I wouldn't be humiliated by attending any regimented meeting of that neo- fascist, paramilitary organization!"

"Oh, I see," Walt said, shaking his head and continuing down the hall with the kids.

Once during a band rehearsal in which he played electric piano, Nathan informed me he was going to immediately report me to the superintendent for my "too professional" expectations for the band, and my strict enforcement of rehearsal attendance. I quickly invited him from the room and said, "Sure Nathan, let's go together right now. The superintendent is a good friend and bowling buddy of mine. He and his wife like to dance at the club where I play. I certainly wouldn't want to keep him waiting." Nathan suddenly decided to postpone his complaint for a later date.

40. A Star Is Born

As any high school coach will agree, it's not unusual to make last-minute substitutions. One holiday concert, a drummer who was totally blind and played in one of my three performing ensembles (we'll name him Eddie) decided to go on strike. You must realize, Eddie had a profanity ridden vocabulary that would easily shame a strip joint comic. He announced loudly backstage that he didn't care if the audience was waiting for him to come out on stage or not, he damned sure wasn't going out there; and furthermore, if we made him go on the #%@! stage, he'd "pee on the audience!"

Not wishing to submit our loyal following to such an impromptu discomfort, I decided to replace "The Mouth" on the spot. I'm not sure what went wrong, but what followed was priceless. Juan, a small but powerful thirteen-year-old, had been playing conga drums in the band all year. He had no usable vision, and I'd allowed him to sit in on the drum set on the numerous times Eddie was in the doghouse. Some of Juan's relatives were in the audience that night, and when I told him he could play the drums for the show, I thought he might explode with excitement. He did remarkably well through the first tune, keeping the beat and listening to my soft instructions as the group played an instrumental ballad. The second selection was a fast, new arrangement of an old rock standard I'd worked out for the band, and I was very concerned Juan might not be able to make it through the tune without pooping out or falling apart rhythmically.

O Contrare Mi Amigo! Two-thirds of the way through, I heard a tremendous banging and crashing of cymbals and drums, sounding very much like someone had stampeded Bertha the elephant through the drum room of a large music store. For no apparent reason, Juan had decided it was time for him to take a drum solo. It made no difference at the moment that he'd never in his life taken a solo before, nor that he wasn't remotely aware of where all the peripheral pieces of the drum set were located. I'm sure now that he had every intention of eventually finding out. His impromptu improvisation continued as the band gradually fell apart, much like the parts of an old car clunking down the highway, one piece falling off at a time. First a muffler, then a bumper, then perhaps a hubcap, next a transmission— you get the picture. Finally, all that remained was me gritting my teeth, smiling valiantly while I continued to bang the chords out on background rhythm guitar. When I finally bit the bullet and realized our musical ship had gone under by the bow, I stopped playing. But the solo roared on! "Ringo" was oblivious of anything else existing in the western world. I'd already asked Juan to stop three times, but it was like shouting in the teeth of a hurricane. The noise from the tortured drums was so ear splitting, Juan either didn't hear me or suddenly decided to also become hearing impaired.

I turned off my guitar, placed it in its stand, pushed back my chair, and found my folding cane. Fumbling around behind the keyboards, I tried to comfort the other confused musicians, while the audience hooted and howled with laughter, clapping loudly in appreciation of Juan's efforts. His percussive offerings had been going on for at least five minutes, or possibly two hours, when I finally made it to the drum set at the back of the stage. Gently. I searched for Juan's arms and found his flailing hands. One at a time, I amputated his drumsticks. I thought it interesting that even though I'd removed his weapons, his feet continued to stomp on the bass drum and high-hat cymbals pedal with amazing ferocity. I signaled the stagehands to pull the curtains, and I heard scattered boos and jeers as the audience voiced their disapproval of my dastardly deed. Juan fought it to the end. Even after the curtain closed, he continued to hit the cymbals with his fists and stomp on the pedals. I slid his drum seat back so he couldn't reach the drum pedals any longer, and with some help, we removed our reluctant percussionist from his steed.

My friend Gary, another teacher who's always helped with our twice a year concerts, said later, "As I ushered Juan backstage, our young star was sweating profusely, and had a grin on his face like the cat that'd swallowed the prized canary!" For five minutes of glory, he had been a rock star. Actually, from the audience's reaction, for a short time I considered making Juan's solo a permanent part of each show. Unfortunately, due to severe ear and tire damage, I thought about it for at least ten seconds.

41. Moonlighting

Mark was a likeable, almost too energetic teenager. He had enough vision to get around without a long cane, but even with visual aids and magnifiers, developmentally, he was unable to read or write. His wiry body was ravaged from birth defects, but he had a grip of iron, and he limped around with the constant energy of a young colt looking for a fence to breach. He'd been raised by a biker family who was notorious hard partyers. Unfortunately, they had been arrested for drug possession and sales numerous times— a rowdy bunch to be sure. Mark knew every heavy metal rock group, the lead guitarist's name, and when their last CD came out. Though he was quite rough around the edges, Mark was a good example for all of the really challenged kids. He always had a smile on his face and a cheery hello to all he passed. "Hey, Mr. O, what's happenin'," was his usual greeting. "You're happenin'," I always replied.

One afternoon, he told me he was going to the media store with a counselor to buy some on-sale CDs. I told him that since he was going, there's a new jazz CD I'd like him to pick up for me. I told him the title and gave him some money, saying he could keep the change. He said, "No way man, it's yours dude." I'll admit, no matter how many times I discouraged him from saying it, Mike's surfer accent was such a kick, he was the only student in my twenty plus years at C.S.B. who could make me grin by calling me "dude." A few days later, Mark saw me and came into the music building, stopping me in the hall. He said loudly (Mark said everything loudly), "I scored your jams, Mr. O, and I got it on sale, man. I stashed your change in my wallet." At that moment, a teacher with her class and teaching assistant came into the building, heading to the weight room at the end of the hall. One of their students recognized Mark's voice and yelled "Hello Mark." I shook my head in embarrassment and disbelief as he gave me the new CD and the change. At the same time, he shouted over his shoulder to his friend down the hall, "Don't bug me now, man. Me and Mr. O. are doin' a deal!"

Mark certainly wasn't bashful, and though streetwise, wasn't aware of the cultures of the rest of the world. One Halloween afternoon, we were returning from a Fremont Symphony concert at the local city college. Mark had been impressed with the William Tell *Overture*, and said he sure wished he'd been around when that "Ranger" guy wrote that neat song from that old radio show his grandpa had a tape of! I guess my music appreciation class hadn't made a lasting impression on the young rocker.

We were driving in a school van along a large complex of recently built apartments. That part of Fremont, California is predominantly Muslim with many Afghanis, Saudis, and other Middle Eastern immigrants. The students in the van were discussing the Halloween dance at the school that night and what costume they'd wear. Mark voiced his own salty opinion of the DJ that always did the dances. By some strange coincidence, the DJ was the son of one of the school staff.

Suddenly Mark yelled out to the other kids, "Hey trick or treat dudes, that's fresh, check it out!" The full meaning of what happened next wasn't clear to me until we returned to the school and the driver, totally cracking up, filled me in on the details. As soon as Mark yelled to everyone inside, the van slowed for a stoplight. I said earlier that he wasn't at all aware of dress styles of other countries. A man with a full beard was walking down the sidewalk. He was dressed in traditional flowing Arab robe, complete with sandals and headdress. The excitement in Mike's voice rang as rolling down the window he yelled, "Killer, dude. Great costume!"

42. They Got Their Tangs Tongled!

One of the most difficult things to teach younger and even older students that are blind, is the concepts of cause and effect, and why you can say or do some things at one time, but not at another. There's a simple reason for this inability. As they grow up, they don't have the benefit of watching others' facial and body language reactions to their behaviors. They don't learn from visual feedback. Four-fifths of what we learn is through our eyes, but that doesn't imply the blind only learn one fifth of what others do. They just have to absorb the information by the other senses.

One older teenager who once sang in my vocal ensemble was the most courteous, well-mannered fellow you could ever meet. Donald did, however, have one interesting quirk. Often, he'd arrive at the music building early and disappear into the men's room. Not long after he locked the door, a line of filthy oaths and curses would float out into the ozone, and my ears and other exterior body parts (as well as those of others who just happened to walk in) would burn and curl in embarrassment. I'm telling you this young man made our drummer friend, "Peeing Eddie" (mentioned earlier), sound like Billy Graham. His teacher later told me that this was a way for Donald to get out all of his negative emotions and curb the violent outbreaks he had experienced in his younger years. It seemed to work, because when he exited the lavatory, he was instantly transformed to his soft-spoken, saint-like self.

Over the next six months, I befriended Donald and tried a little diversionary tactic. I wasn't sure if it would work, but I figured anything would be an improvement, for the young man couldn't go the rest of his life cussing out every poor soul at Disneyland or McDonalds that happened to drop in to use the can. I know to the person on the street this might sound a little bizarre, but it worked, and the end result was better than the other alternative. We talked about singing when he was angry, instead of cussing. I taught Donald an old ditty a bus driver taught me in the fourth grade. As a kid, I always sang it out loud when I was out of earshot when Anne, my stepmom, was mad at me. It seemed a way to be irreverent and not get in any trouble. Donald loved it and took to it like Bill Clinton to a photo op.

In only weeks, he was singing the tune when he retired to the throne room, instead of his usual vocal garbage. He had a beautiful baritone, and I can still hear him singing behind the door with the resonance of James Earl Jones, "Never throw a lighted lamp at Mother, it's ten to one you'll never have another. Mother wouldn't like to be, lit up like a Christmas tree, so never throw a lighted lamp at Mother."

Pete was another linguistically gifted student, often when angry, and gifted with all the wrong words. He had a run-in one day with an immovable object. I'd just walked in the teachers' lounge hallway to get my mail for my assistant to read to me when a transportation counselor brought Pete in from outside. He was spitting mad, and the young woman with him said to the receptionist, "Pete needs to see Lavorna." Overhearing her name, "L.V.," as we all call her, came out of her office. Picture an articulate, solidly built African American lady, perhaps in her sixties. The consummate professional, no nonsense, but with a heart as big as an aircraft carrier. Don't anyone ever try to mistreat one of our kids when she's around, but don't any student ever try to get away with anything around her either. L.V., the young lady, said, "Pete here has been foul mouthing everything and everybody in the van because he can't get his seat belt fastened. Yet, he won't let anybody help him, and the van is really late getting the students home. The driver said she's not going to allow him to ride if he doesn't have his belt fastened and doesn't clean up his language."

"What's the problem here, Pete? I know you have better manners than that," Lavorna spoke firmly.

"It's that #%@! seatbelt. I can't get my #%@! fingers to snap the #%@! thing shut, and I hate having girls helping me like I'm a #%@! little kid."

"Alright, Pete. First, I'll make it clear. That kind of language isn't welcome here or anyplace else. If you expect to be treated with respect you must respect others. Now let's see if we can fix the problem. What if one of the guys helped you with the belt?"

"Nah, it's the way that #%@! belt holder is designed."

"I said that's enough of that talk, Pete. This is the last time I'm warning you, no more filthy language, you understand? I can't help you until you calm down." Lavorna was doing her magic, and her patience was slowing the big guy down. But I still heard the frustration in his voice as he tried to control his profanity.

"Yeah, but, but it's that seatbelt, that god…"

"Pete! Don't you dare say that!" L.V.'s voice rose this time.

A few seconds of silence passed, then Pete continued, stammering a little, "With nobody helpin', I just want to be able to fasten that…uh…darned…that god…er… that darned…beer-drinking seatbelt!"

For years, Lavorna was my bowling partner on the school team. On more than one occasion when she picked me up after school in her van, smiling, she'd help me with my beer-drinking seatbelt.

43. With hands like that, Kid, you'll never play the guitar.

The violin is one of the smallest of the stringed instruments, but one of the finest bluegrass fiddlers I ever heard was six-foot-seven and weighed nearly four hundred pounds. I never make evaluations or teaching decisions on the information of others, until I've done my own evaluations and assessments. I've learned from personal experience not to judge or predict the possibilities of a student's eventual success without a lengthy period of evaluation and trial and error. The latter sometimes is the best indicator of which direction to go.

When I was thirteen, I went to a well-known guitar teacher in the community to take lessons. Floyd, my "step-dad," was an accomplished welder, and when I was five years old and full of curiosity, I managed to get into his welding supplies in the garage. I found a jar of mercury and opened the heavy container, fascinated with the silvery mobile liquid metal. An hour later, I'd gotten a large amount of it in my mouth and all over my fingers and hands. Within hours, I was violently ill, and the folks rushed me to the hospital. I'd given myself a healthy case of mercury poisoning and was in the hospital for nearly a month. I was a very sick welder. The lasting effects of the poisoning were nervous shaking spasms in my hands, and muscle jerks in the large muscles of my arms and legs. I have them to this day, but have learned to control them, and unless I'm unusually nervous, the small hand tremors aren't noticeable.

Using its cardboard box as a case, I took my twenty-dollar Stella guitar Anne had bought me at Wards and eagerly headed to the music store for my first guitar lesson. Like every other thirteen-year-old at the time, I wanted to sing and play like Elvis and impress my friends. I remember the teacher as if he were sitting next to me at this moment. He was in his late twenties, impatient, and not very friendly. It was obvious even to a kid that he hated teaching beginners and felt his talents would be better showcased on stage (singing like Elvis and impressing his friends). After only ten minutes, "Mr. Encouragement" took the guitar from me and replaced it in its box, "Give this to your brother or a friend, kid. With hands as shaky as those, you'll never play the guitar."

I think I cried the rest of the day, and then became angry. I had Anne buy me some instruction records, and I attacked that poor plywood guitar like Jessie Ventura assaulting a sausage pizza. I distinctly remember having to put Band-Aids on the ends of my bleeding fingers after a few days, but I refused to give up.

Ten years later, the teacher was working at another studio. I took him a spin-off of a tape of me and an electric bass player playing the jazz classic, "Take Five" with Joe Morello (Dave Brubeck's drummer on the original fifties jazz recording). Joe had been hired to teach a day for a percussion seminar at a large local music school, where I'd just been hired to teach guitar. Upon presenting the tape, I reminded my old "would-be" teacher of my first and only lesson I ever took. He was very confused when I told him he should be proud. It was the best lesson anyone ever gave. I learned enough in ten minutes to help me for the rest of my life!

44. Disgruntled Employer

Rolf was another memorable student of mine. Born in Lebanon, he entered C.S.B. in his late teens and spoke English with a thick accent. Rolf was another of those special kids that often confounded their teachers. He didn't read or write, had minimal academic skills, but could speak four languages fluently: Farsi, Croatian, Arabic, and English; and he could memorize melodies and lyrics with uncanny skill.

One holiday concert, we performed the piece, "Missa Criola," by Ramirez, a modern South American composer. At the beginning of the semester, I gave Rolf a CD of the work and asked him to memorize the vocal solos for the first two songs on the recording so we could teach the choir the background vocal parts. It was a three-day weekend. Rolf came back on Tuesday and had the entire work, solos and choruses, all thirty-two minutes of it, totally memorized. If this wasn't amazing enough, the entire recording was in Spanish! His mother told me later, Rolf had only been exposed to Spanish since they'd moved to California the year before. By the time he left C.S.B. five years later, he could also converse both in Spanish and Italian.

The sad reality of Rolf's situation was that due to his poor social and cognitive skills, we were unable to find employment for him as an interpreter or language coach where he could use his special gift. Most of the sighted public doesn't realize that many students with vision problems have them in companion with, or as a result of, other more debilitating medical conditions. During my years at the school, I've had at least a dozen or more students weighing barely over a pound at birth. Often, the critical areas of the brain and nervous system develop normally, but sometimes (and for a number of medical reasons) they do not.

Rolf may have had some unfortunate challenges, but he was not a fool. I always played guitar at recess, and the kids would gather around and sing songs, calling out their favorites. One morning, I was surprised to find him sitting next to me, singing in his fine baritone voice. After the song, I asked him, "Hey Rolf, how come you're here today? Aren't you supposed to be working at the workshop off campus?" I knew he and some other older students went four days a week to a work site near Santa Clara where they worked on projects for United Airlines and other carriers. They stuffed envelopes, bagged earphones, and separated small, used electronic and building components to be melted down or recycled.

"They asked me to quit," came his heavily accented answer. "I didn't like my job."

"Oh yeah, Rolf, what did they have you doing on your job?" Later, I learned from another teacher that the students at that jobsite sorted titanium and aluminum screws and rivets (taken from mountings and equipment in the company's aircraft, which were in a constant state of maintenance).

"I had to put the square screws in the square box, and the round screws in the round can."

"Why did they make you stay back here at school?" I asked, genuinely curious. I didn't have to see to know a smile was on his face as he announced slowly and with devilish satisfaction in his voice, "I kept putting the round screws in the square box."

45. Do you hear what I see?

Some of the funniest things I've experienced occurred while traveling. Once while riding on the rapid transit train without my guide dog, I had my folding cane tucked next to me and was listening to some sounds on my MP3 player. Suddenly I felt a hand gently touch my shoulder, and I looked up to face in the direction of the person, as I always teach my students to do. I felt a movement in the air but didn't know what was going on. A few seconds later, I felt another firmer touch on my sleeve, and by now was getting a little annoyed. Then, hearing a series of guttural sounds in front of me, I realized the person standing there was gesturing because he was hearing impaired. I held up my hand and finger-spelled to the young-sounding man that I was blind myself. He roared a great laugh at our predicament and stuck a small American flag pin into my shirt pocket. He'd obviously been selling them to the riders on the train. I reached in a pocket for my wallet, but he shook my shoulder warmly and walked away as I then laughed, too. It took only seconds to realize the humor and improbability of our encounter.

I still take graduate classes and love to learn about the new innovations in technology in education. A few years ago, I walked out of a graduate class where I'd just delivered a guest lecture to prospective teachers and walked down the hall to a class I was taking on computer assistive technology. Later that evening, I was deep in thought, waiting for the bus near the entrance of San Francisco State University. When the bus rolled up, folks began boarding in a rush. Suddenly, someone in front of me was pulling on the end of my long cane. Gamely, I tried to pull it back, it was mine, and I was hungry and tired. Darn it, if they wanted to play cane, they'd have to get one of their own. Besides, I didn't have a replacement on board my person. I soon took this match on as a personal challenge, something akin to a blind guy tug-of-war. I was ready to bet my only set of Braille dice they weren't goin' to win this one. Finally, after a few rousing choruses of the theme from "Rocky," someone next to me laughing said, "It's okay man, he's just trying to help you. He's a foreign fellow and he's trying to pull you on the bus!"

Airports, public transportation, restaurants, and large gatherings are fertile ground for "Oh my, Edith, did you see what that man did?" situations, and general screw-ups. But they're also good spots for an occasional teaching moment for the public. Some years ago, I was playing solo in Santa Clara for the formal dinner of a large convention. After an hour or so of playing, a sweet-sounding lady came on stage and informed me that now was a good time to take a break, for they were about to do a drawing for some fine door prizes. Minutes later, a man came by our table selling raffle tickets. My wife Janet had stepped out of the room for a while, and I wasn't wearing sunglasses, nor was my cane in sight. He asked if I wanted to buy some tickets. I said sure and asked how much they were. He said, "A buck apiece, or six for five bucks."

"That's a deal, give me six." I pulled out my wallet and searched for a five-dollar bill. Nearly all who are blind have their own way of folding and identifying paper money. I fold my fives in half, tens in quarters long-ways, and twenties in quarters like a five folded twice. As I felt and unfolded the bill, handing it to the man, he must have seen that my eyes weren't focusing on his.

He stuttered a bit and then blurted, "Oh, I'm sorry! I didn't know you're blind. I guess you'll have to get a normal sighted person to read these tickets for you." Grinning, there was no way I could let that one slide.

"Damn", I answered without hesitation, "I was really hoping to find an abnormal one to help me out."

Rarely a day goes by that something a little off the wall doesn't happen. It might be something as simple as on a bus, someone not answering when I ask, "is anyone sitting in this seat?" If there's no answer, I usually end up roosting in their lap before they protest in affront, finding I've made some very up-close contact with their person. I've found it's a happening way to meet new friends. I've been tempted on occasion to ask the ladies for the next dance, but usually after I've moved my two-octave spread from their laps, we're both too embarrassed to talk. I've noticed over the years buses seem to be a fine stage for some amusing and bizarre situations.

46. The Butt Stops Here!

Rarely a week passes where I don't join in as a cast member of a comedy episode that proves to be a head-scratcher or good for a laugh. Often the folks with whom we interact don't have much more of a clue how to handle a situation any better than we do. The following is a perfect example of the most direct solution to an immediate problem. Now remember, you're the blind person and you don't see what's coming.

Once, as I climbed on a city bus, I expected the usual events I'd experienced a thousand times before. When you don't see, after years of riding buses and talking to drivers, you get to become a second-hand expert on buses, their power plants, models, reliability, seating arrangements, and the other drivers' love lives, but thankfully, not much about "Beer drinking seatbelts." I wasn't ready for the surprise waiting for me on the bus on this day.

It was burning up outside, with no shade to share, and the dozen riders at the bus stop were particularly irritated and grouchy. A child of six was whimpering and hiding behind its grandma, afraid of my dog guide, and the bus was twenty minutes late. Near the rear of the group, a young woman's uncomfortable baby had decided to scream the last act of Wagner's "Flying Dutchman," while some jackass (much like me fifteen years earlier), apparently oblivious of those around him, paced on the far side, puffing furiously on an expensive cigar. Perhaps he was trying to combust the rest of it before someone murdered him or the bus arrived. I have a theory, quite the opposite of what one might think; the rarer the tobacco in a hand-rolled cigar, the more it stinks! The diminutive coloratura singing her heroic role from her stroller, finished the last cadenza at the end of her aria as the bus rolled up in a noxious cloud of diesel gases, dust, and screeching brakes.

I lay back waiting for the women and younger kids to get aboard, hoping Fidel Castro and his stink stick were forever separated from their oral bliss. I remember a woman speaking to me in a foreign language sounding Slavic, but for some reason, that day I couldn't understand a word. Finally, Oliver, my guide dog at the time, and I climbed aboard.

There were still folks in front of me when we reached the top step, so I waited patiently for the line to recede. Many of the boarding riders were complaining to the poor lady driver, and I heard from the din around us, the bus was very full. I soon began entertaining the possibility Ollie and I might end up standing. If sitting was not a possibility, standing was far superior to the other option, lying down!

Slowly the grumbling folks paid their fares and moved to the rear and then I heard a young man softly say to me as he touched my arm and stood up. "Here man, take my seat, there's one more a few rows back." Evidently the harried bus driver was not aware of the young fellow's remark, and was eager to get the troops rolling, for I felt and heard her jump up from the driver's seat. Holding out my ID bus pass I was confronted by a nearly six-foot, African American woman of perhaps forty years of age (from the sound of her voice). Unceremoniously, she faced me, grabbed both my shoulders with her powerful hands, spun me around, and pushed me back toward the just vacated seat. As she spoke in a stressed but kind voice, she firmly placed me down into the seat. "Here, baby, you sit here!"

At that wonderful teaching moment, the only words that dribbled out of my gaping mouth were, "Uh, yes ma'am, thank you, thank you very much."

47. To Hell with People who can't take a Joke!

For a few years before he transferred to the South Bay, I was befriended by an Alameda County Transit bus driver named Stan. Near the top in driver's seniority, he was a burly ex-Marine probably in his middle fifties. Stan tolerated no clandestine or subversive activity from anyone on his bus. One afternoon while I rode into Alameda with him, I almost jumped out of my underwear, startled by his drill-sergeant voice as he roared at some offenders in the rear. After some minutes had elapsed since he'd given his foghorn warning to two young men who'd fired up a joint in the back of his coach, Stan pulled over and switched off the engine. Slowly he got up and walked to the back. The only words I heard were the curses of the two youths, as he unceremoniously threw both of them out the back door.

I knew Stan was a little off center in some ways, but he had a great sense of humor. On a particular day after work, when my guide dog was at the vet for an illness, I walked up to board his bus to Alameda. It was crowded because a San Francisco train had just come in on the Rapid Transit. I was wearing a school windbreaker that read "Staff" across the back and was tapping my white cane. I made my way onto the bus after letting the folks in front of me go first. As I climbed the last step, from the driver's seat Stan announced in a loud irritated voice, "Well Wayne, it's about damned time you showed up for my relief, you know my split started fifteen minutes ago, these folks got to get home." He jumped out of his seat, and to my surprise, he spun me around, seating me in the driver's seat. Of course, the engine wasn't running, and the brakes were set. But I swear as Stan stepped outside lighting a cigarette, at least three or four passengers were right behind him! He roared with laughter, and I stood up to find my rightful place. After he finished his smoke, we were on our way. A few of the unsuspecting passengers didn't appreciate the humor, for I remember a few weeks later, the spontaneous joke cost Stan a day's suspension.

I may joke about some of the encounters those of us with disabilities experience, but I don't fault the sighted public. Often, the only reason these incidents occur is that the public is not educated or informed, or I've not explained myself loudly or clearly enough. I teach my students that often when they find themselves in a predicament, the reason some folks don't jump in to help is their own self-consciousness and not wanting to embarrass you or themselves, or just plain curiosity to see how you'll handle the situation. Their hesitancy to help is rarely from lack of caring. It's tough for all of us to not take an occasional rebuke or insult personally, but there isn't a sighted, non-disabled person alive who hasn't run into a jerk or two in their life

48. Up Speak!

I'm sure there must be many others in the community who are as sensitive to those with disabilities (or "unique gifts", as I've sometimes referred to them) as we are, but my wife Jan and I have always tried our best to be sensitive to the space and dignity of others. Jan is severely dyslexic, her Goddaughter is hearing impaired, and her oldest son has the use of only one arm, a result of a horrific motorcycle accident. The following experience is a great example of the subconscious mind overriding one's mouth, further substantiating my hero and his first rule of social interaction. Here is "Dr. Credos Gumperson's Rule #5: The most active mouth requires insertion of the largest foot.

A few years ago, we'd just finished remodeling our kitchen, as well as other large rooms in our 1920's Mediterranean home. My beautiful wife Jan is an amazing and sensitive woman. Not only is she a Cordon Bleu chef, but also an award-winning fashion designer and interior decorator. Her remake of the front room of that same house won a large cash prize in a national contest hosted by *Ladies Home Journal* (Hey, how's that for winning a brandied filet with cheese tortellini for dinner after she reads this?).

Robert, a wonderful young man working in the office with my wife, and his brother had been responsible for many of the Architectural drawings. We invited both Robert and his brother over to the house one afternoon to have a drink and to see the final results of the remodeling, for we were truly grateful for the work he'd added to the project. Robert and his brother arrived a half-hour late, as was Robert's custom, a sign of a true artist (or "flake," in my "dad's" opinionated vernacular). One of the unique features of Robert and his brother Phillip was their statures. Robert was less than five feet, and Phillip was not much more than four feet, at best. From the moment they drove up, I swear as I sit in front of this computer, every word that issued from my mouth seemed to have something to do with size, height, or dimensions. The more we were aware of the fact, the worse it got. "Oh hello, you two, hope you had a pleasant little drive, and didn't have to take any detours or short-cuts. Come on inside for a bit and we'll have a wee drink. Maybe you'd prefer a half split of champagne, or maybe a short beer before we get you a little something to eat. Okay now, come up here and go down into the kitchen, then in a short while, we'll go below to the basement and we'll see what the carpenters have been up to." Well, it wasn't quite that bad, but close. After we went into the kitchen, and I had invited them to sit down, I vowed to keep my mouth shut. Against the corner of the room near the entrance of the downstairs hall, we had a small Irish wood-burning stove sitting on a half-foot raised stone platform. Phillip squatted and sat on the stones, crossing his legs like a marionette.

Jan once told me a story about a tiny lady she'd costumed for an upcoming movie photo shoot while working for a prestigious costume company in San Francisco. Jan couldn't help it, but at one point while the little woman sat with her legs crossed smoking a cigarette, Jan moved her entire person around to adjust an alteration on the diminutive lady's attire. A miniature volcano erupted right there on the counter, and Jan, not realizing her faux pas, was soundly and rightly rebuked. Jan said that when Phillip sat down on the hearth, she had that same urge to pick him up and play "tea party" with him!

But the beauty of the human spirit is that as soon as we're together for any length of time, the differences and traits making us unique become positive contributors to the appreciation of the whole person. Of course, the strikingly beautiful person will always be noticed, but the most plain or unattractive individual becomes a candidate for a museum portrait of art when they sing, act, or play music with a passion that moves our most stolid emotions. "How about a tiny bit more coffee, Robert? Are you ready for a fill up? We wish you could have stayed longer. Oh, I'm sorry Phillip, I should've put that Collins in a tall glass." I suppose for the first time, I truly understood how uncomfortable people feel when they catch themselves using sighted terms talking to a blind person. I say, "Who cares, we're all in this passage together. And besides, God's watching and deserves a good show!"

49. Back-To-School, Two-for-One Sale!

For a few years at CSB, I had the genuine treat of teaching twin twelve-year-old brothers. Totally blind, Ricky and Justin were almost completely identical except for a slight difference in the timbre of their voices. Daily, most everyone got them confused. They were tall and slim, fair-haired and precocious, and for the most part due to their energy level, a full-time career for anyone attempting to teach them on a daily basis. Both boys often showed the "right word, wrong place" behavior mentioned earlier. I thought I had the exclusive patent on this skill: turning up the volume of the football game in church before making sure the earphones are plugged in! But after teaching some of my outspoken charges for a few years, I know now the ability to not think ahead at the repercussions of your actions is not solely mine.

To truly understand these complex students, one has to spend a lot of time around them and see the warmth and thirst for information most of them exhibit daily. I've always tried to think of the students not as blind, but different in a positive way. One of my biggest disagreements with what many blind children are told, is the misconception, "You're no different than anyone else. You can do anything you want if you try hard enough." Perhaps it sounds realistic to those who say the phrase, and the concept is noble and wonderful indeed; however, in truth, the statement is a crock! Difference is gauged only in the eyes of the beholder, measured by their personal standards. The blind are different. We can't see. Yao Ming is different; he's seven feet six inches tall. But being unique has some wonderful and exciting facets. Their "disability" makes them learn and experience the world in exciting new and individual ways. Being unique is a positive thing. It's only a liability if we allow it to be.

Ricky and Justin sang in the Glee Club, an afternoon singing group at the school. I often would take this group out to retirement homes, hospitals, and other public performances for a variety of reasons: it's fun for them and gives them a feeling of giving something back to the community, it's a great social experience, meeting the public, the simple fact they're good and enthusiastic singers. One evening during the holiday season, we traveled to the Masonic Home in Fremont to perform. We were met at the entrance by two elderly gentlemen sent to assist us to the hall where we were to sing. As we walked, I heard one of the men start a conversation with one of the twins. The man had a deep, rolling bass voice and said, "So your name is Justin. How old are you? My name's Joe, young man."

"I'm eleven, and I gotta friend named Joe too,", Justin said, "but his voice isn't as low as yours. How old are you?"

"I'm ninety-one years old," the man said proudly.

"No way, Joe!" Justin blurted out in amazement. "That's impossible. Ain't nobody that old!" Trying to teach the students proper answers to questions and proper responses to various situations, is a never-ending task. There's always plenty of student-generated ammunition for the teaching cannon.

At the end of that school year, my associate music teacher and mentor was retiring after nearly thirty years of teaching at the School for the Blind. She loved classical music, and I'm sure, often looked with suspicion at the modern "jazzy" approach to my teaching. The superintendent called a school-wide assembly for her retirement ceremony and asked me to sing something operatic for her; I was delighted to do so. Another staff member was a fine pianist accompanied me on the haunting tenor aria from *The Elixir of Love,* "Una Furtiva Lagrima." I sang it with all the Italian passion and feeling I could muster, holding the high notes, surely feeling I was approaching the artistic mastery of Pavarotti or Andrea Bocelli. There was silence for a few seconds after the applause, and I knew from the sound of her "thank you" that my retiring colleague had tears in her eyes. Then a clear young voice floated from the rear of the theater. Ricky, the blunter of the twins, said, "I love you Mr. O, but that music sucks!"

50. Taking on The Challenge

Whether they want to admit it or not, every teacher at some point in their career has special or "favorite" students. I've always said that the true measure of a professional teacher is their ability to teach the students with whom they don't particularly identify with the same enthusiasm and dedication as those to whom they're naturally drawn.

I fell in teaching love with Matthew the very first time we met. In addition to his blindness, Matt was born with many orthopedic and physical challenges. During his early development in the womb, certain parts and surfaces of his body became attached to the lining of his mother's uterine walls and didn't develop properly. Matt was born with no eyes, few facial features, only half a thumb and pinky finger on his left hand, and no first joint or fingernails on the right. The brave young man endured many progressive surgeries as he approached his teens to rebuild his facial structures, nose, and mouth. My wife years later said the surgeons that helped Matt were unbelievable in their skill, for by the time he left our school, his features were quite becoming. You can imagine my dismay and discomfort when ten-year-old Matthew came in the music room soon after I'd met him and told me in an excited tone, "I want to play the guitar just like you!" I may have mentioned earlier, I never tell a student "no," only that we will give it a try and see what happens. I told Matt about the great Belgian jazz guitarist, Django Rinehart, who, as a boy, was trapped in a fire and lost a finger and half of another on his fretting hand. For the next few days, I racked my brain for a workable way to approach our problem. Then, I came up with an idea.

A musician friend of mine had donated a half-sized Brazilian nylon string guitar to the school the year before. Reversing the nut so it could be restrung left-handed, I put a set of light tension strings on it (exactly the same technique I'd used years earlier for the GI with only one arm) and lowered the string action, making it easier to fret. I taught Matthew to pick the strings with an up stroke of his half little finger of his left hand. Very slowly over a period of weeks, we worked on building up some callouses on the tender fingertips of his right hand. The bones at the tips of his fingers were just beneath the surface of the skin. In a short time, his stubby little fingers began to spread out enough that he could play four frets in a row up and down the fingerboard of the guitar. He soon learned to strum the strings with his left half-little finger, but I knew he'd never be able to pick the single strings with any speed unless I came up with something different. The one night, I sat up in bed, and a light came on in my foggy brain. The next day, I took a large mandolin flat pick over to a buddy of mine in the maintenance department of the school. I had him heat the plastic and bend it around so the curve would fit the space near the base of Matt's half-thumb. Then, I asked him to drill a small hole in the middle of the pick, and through the hole, I ran an eight-inch length of nylon guitar string knotted into a loop (these strings are very similar to thick nylon fishing line).

I had Matt put his wrist through the loop and grip the pick with his half-thumb and half-pinky. He had to pick with his wrist sticking out at a severe angle, but in just a few weeks, he was flying up and down the frets. His new pick allowed him to play notes on both the up and down strokes of his picking hand. Every time he dropped the pick, the nylon loop kept it from falling on the floor, and he could quickly retrieve it with his other hand. Six months later in his first concert, I backed him up on rhythm guitar as he played on a Gibson Les Paul Jr. the beautiful melody of the ballad, "Hello," by Lionel Ritchie. A year later Matthew was playing electric guitar in our middle skill band, the Mission Ensemble.

We both loved sports, but he could tell you who played second base for the Mets ten years ago, and what the guy's batting average was. He was very verbal, with a great vocabulary. I nearly fell out of my chair when after only a few lessons, I asked him how he thought he did on a song he'd just tried to play. The ten-year-old answered in a serious, matter of fact tone, "Well, Mr. Oliver, I thought it was mediocre."

On many occasions, tapping his cane and walking away down the hall after his lesson, Matt would leave me with tears in my eyes. I often thanked God for giving me the opportunity to teach him. At this writing, Matt has graduated with honors from my old alma mater, San Jose State University. Hail to that Spartan!

51. Hey Man, Keep Brushin' Those Canines!

I thought I'd preface this next section with a few words of explanation about guide dogs to clear up any misconceptions or answer some of the most common questions folks have asked me about them. Dogs selected to become "dog guides," as they're called these days, are indeed special animals, wonderful examples of beauty, temperament, behavior, and trainability. The relatively few breeds used today are selected for various reasons including longevity, health patterns and history, adaptability to weather and climate, and of course, intelligence. Most of the training schools across the country now have their own kennels and breeding lines. Many of the pups are raised away from the school for a length of time by 4-H members or other selected volunteers, who train the puppies in their own homes, teaching them basic people skills: sociability, housebreaking, and simple commands (sit, stay etc.). Then, they are returned to the training school for many months of extensive and concentrated training. Gradually, the dogs not suitable as guides are separated from the program. At the end of their training, the remaining guide dog candidates are placed with prospective blind companions or "handlers", who spend at least three to four weeks at the site with the dog, twenty-four hours a day, seven days a week. The schools are usually in a residential setting where the prospective companion of the dog stays until they learn to work as a team.

Here are some things to know about guide dogs. Whenever you see a harnessed dog walking in public on the left side of someone, it is more than likely a guide dog. It is a means of mobility and freedom for the blind person and helps them to be more comfortable in strange surroundings. The dog is not intended to protect the handler from personal attack, but as with any other dog, would more than likely do this if the occasion arose. It is rare for attack, harnessed guard, or search dogs to be seen intermingling with the public, except of course at airports or security risk locations. So, when you find yourself close to a harnessed dog, it is almost surely a gentle guide dog.

Only a small percentage of the blind have guide dogs for various reasons. Not everyone is a "dog person". Perhaps someday we'll have guide pigs, gooney birds, or guide alligators, but as of yet, the concept hasn't quite caught on. I'll admit, there's been a few times when I've had to play music in some parts of town where a good guide alligator would have been an asset. The dogs require a great deal of constant attention, including grooming, medical check-ups and follow-up care, exercise, relieving, and feeding. As with most other dogs, guide dogs become very attached to their owners, and aren't usually allowed to run free over wide outside areas for long periods of time. Their behavior is structured and controlled in public when they're in harness, but when the harness is off, they can be just as dopey and playful as any other housedog.

Though they are wonderful, loving animals, both helpers and trusted companions, they are not pets. To the blind, the guide dog becomes nearly indispensable after only a few months. Over the years, I've found I can travel so much faster and safer with my guide dog than with my cane. Living in the San Francisco Bay Area, we get a good deal of rain over the year, and the outside sound along the streets can get very distorted and loud when traffic plows through water. You can't feel a car about to hit you in noisy traffic with a cane tip on the ground!

The term "owner" is becoming unacceptable for those with guide dogs. There is a movement afoot not to use the term any longer, having to do with animal rights. The term "handler" has become the common replacement. Rarely a week goes by without someone refusing to get in an elevator with me, for fear of my guide dog. Never be afraid of a harnessed guide. The dogs are specifically bred to be docile and friendly to the public. Any animal demonstrating aggressive or biting behavior is immediately removed from the training programs. Guide dogs aren't blessed with a sixth sense. They do not have magical powers, nor do they read the owner's mind. I'm not trying to be flippant. The public has asked these questions of me more than once. Nearly all their behaviors and skills are taught over months of training and the countless repetition of behaviors and commands until the dog has the skill imprinted in their behavior. They don't read stoplights. They learn to move with the direction and flow of traffic patterns and sidewalk configurations. When the handler is in a strange area, the dog must be told which direction to go: right, left, or forward. If the dog knows the route, it will more than likely take its handler the entire way without any prompting, stopping for obstacles above or on the sidewalk. But, if at some point along the way the blind person wants to go a different direction, the dog must be commanded to do so. Nine times out of ten when we goof up in some way or another, I'll give you one guess who is to blame for the "uh-oh, this doesn't work."

Though most of their skills are taught by repetition and patterning, they are still uncanny creatures, and never cease to amaze me with their intelligence and memory. They can on command, lead you to the phone, traffic light buttons on crossing poles, drinking fountains, stairs and elevators, bus and taxi stops, and a myriad of other things. They can pick up things you drop: keys; coins; transit tickets; steak sandwiches; and of course, beer-drinking seat belts. If I win your selection, you show remarkable insight. In the next few pages, I've recounted some interesting and humorous things I've experienced with my dogs over the years. Grab a biscuit from the container in the kitchen and curl up on the couch. I hope you don't doze off for at least five minutes, and by the way, no licking 'til later!

52. Shaunessy

My first guide dog was a beautiful reddish blond retriever who I immediately renamed Shaunessy, after the drummer in Doc Severinsen's band on the old "Tonight Show," with Johnny Carson. Every owner knows how different each dog they've had can be, and Shaunessy was no exception. He was big, whippy, and had a nearly human personality. My friends said he had huge brown eyes, and I think I must've spent at least the combined hours of a military career combing and grooming his silky coat. I never allowed him to do it on rainy days when he was wet, but often when we climbed on the bus, if it wasn't crowded, he'd hop his rump up on the seat next to me with his front paws on the floor and sit like a regular passenger.

Fitting his name, I gave him an Irish golf hat on which I attached an elastic band. He wore it for years and would often bring it to me when he wanted it on. I've long ago cleaned up my act, but at that time, I smoked a pipe, and more than once when my wife would pick me up at the BART (commuter train) station in Oakland, she'd find him sitting next to me, wearing my sunglasses, his hat at a rakish angle, with my Meerschaum pipe in his mouth. His nasty smoking habit didn't seem to have an adverse effect on his health, for he lived to be nearly sixteen. He had a habit of doing things I never expected, but always kept me safe (though often shaking my head). Jan also admitted he was something special and called him my "Guide Jester."

One afternoon I was late for a private party I'd been hired to play and was rushing down a wide sidewalk on Broadway in Oakland, headed for the restaurant near the bay where the party was to be. I carried my guitar in my right hand, and my big, blond buddy was hooking it big-time as he often did. Suddenly I felt him move slightly to the left, and assumed he'd just walked me around something on the sidewalk. We'd only walked a few more steps when I heard a stream of curses erupt from someone behind me. "Hey, man, your #%@! dog stole my bird!"

I jerked to a stop, not understanding what was going on. I turned and questioned, "I'm sorry, what did you say?"

"I told you, man, your damn dog just ate my chicken. He's still got it in his mouth!" The man had evidently been sitting on a bench in front of the park, and when we passed by, Shaunessy must've thought the man was offering him a treat for good work and removed the gift from the man's hand as he passed by. I was soon five bucks lighter, as I paid the man for his pilfered KFC. Unfortunately, I couldn't let my felonious rogue enjoy the fruits of his crime, so I took the chicken from him and tossed it to the animals in the park. Sadly, I noticed a definite loss of spring in his step the rest of the way.

53. Jeepjack in the Morning

With the help of some relatives and friends, I was able to hock my first born, get some business loans, and pool my small savings enough to buy the music store where I'd been working for the past eight years. Next-door was a large post office facility. Behind it was parked an extensive pool of delivery jeeps and other vehicles. I have to preface what follows by saying I have the deepest respect and admiration for the hard working and dedicated employees of the U.S. Postal Service. The actions of one person have certainly not tarnished my feelings.

One afternoon, I'd taken Shaunessy out the rear of the hall behind my store to relieve himself. I always keep small bells on my dogs' collars, because that way I always know where they are when they are off harness. I heard him trotting away toward the fence near the rear of the post office next door, so I called for him to come back. There was silence for a second, then I heard the gruff voice of a man at the rear landing of the post office cursing loudly at my dog: "You let that #%@! mutt pee on my tires again, and I'll kill the #%@!!"

A little embarrassed, I yelled, "I'm sorry. I can't see, and I didn't know he was close to your vehicle." Two days later from inside my store, I heard tires screeching outside, and a few seconds later a mom and her young daughter came into the studio for the little girl's lesson.

"Some creep from the post office nearly ran over us with his jeep as he was leaving the back-parking lot behind the building. It was really close!" The woman was obviously shaken, and it wasn't the first time someone had complained about the way a driver from next door tore out of the driveway between the two buildings. This time, I decided to call the postmaster next door and tell him my concerns. The woman had written down the number of the jeep, and I related it to the postmaster explaining how many youngsters came in and out of my studio and store during summer vacation. He promised he'd check into it and talk to the driver. The following Monday, the angry driver came in just after lunch, cursing me and saying I'd gotten him in trouble with his boss with my complaints, saying I was just getting even for him yelling at my dog. I explained I didn't even know it was him driving the jeep the woman had complained about. But it did no good, for he stormed out, saying I'd better not count on getting my mail on time from now on. Shaunessy had been sitting next to me during the entire shouting scene, and I felt him quivering, not understanding what was happening.

The very next morning, I arrived an hour early to open the store. I had a glass repair man sitting in his truck waiting to replace one of the store windows. A budding Barry or Bretta Bonds at the park next door had broken it with a baseball earlier that morning. To my surprise, a jeep came careening around the corner of the building at high speed and screeched to a stop in front of the entrance of my store. The driver of the glass truck later explained everything that happened next. The postman snapped a large rubber band around my mail and tossed it out the open door of the jeep, saying, "Here's your damn mail!"

I'd been in the process of trying to find my burglar alarm and front door key to let the glass man in, and Shaunessy had been waiting at my side. As Shaunessy saw the bundle of mail come flying toward us and hit the ground, he retrieved it and galloped toward the jeep to return it from where it'd come. He jumped up into the open passenger side of the jeep the driver had opened. At the same time, the mailman beat a hasty retreat out the driver's door, leaving the jeep still running. Shaunessy promptly sat down in the driver's seat with the mail bundle in his mouth, as though waiting to see what was next. The irate postman jumped up and down, cursing wildly, with the sound of his boots echoing down the parking lot storm drain grating on which he was jumping. He screamed for me to get my #%@! dog out of his jeep. But strangely I was unable to, for suddenly I found it nearly impossible to find my keys. It had become necessary to search every pocket and hiding place on my person for the elusive things. I know I must've been grinning when I heard the glass man roaring with laughter from inside his truck. Finally, after picking up everything I'd placed on the ground to search my pockets, including a large cup of coffee from the doughnut house nearby, I felt my way to the front door and spent the next few minutes fumbling with the burglar alarm switch I'd reset earlier that morning (after adding one baseball to my store's modest inventory). It's amazing how one can forget a learned skill from one day to the next. After I finally opened the door, I whistled for Richard Petty, still sitting behind the wheel. He immediately bounded from the jeep still holding my mail in his mouth. Laughing, the glass man came in the store entrance behind me, and the last thing I heard was the squeal of burning rubber as the jeep left the scene.

54. Get Your Priorities Straight

One of my adult students, Bob, bought a beautiful young Dalmatian. The problem was the dog was a magnificent animal, but as wild as the wind. After a few months of trying to train him himself, Bob surrendered with honor and enrolled "Jake" in a Saturday afternoon obedience class, sponsored by the local SPCA. After about a month, I asked Bob how his dog was doing, and he assured me the training had made a world of difference: the "bundle of energy" had cut down his shoe-eating habit to only three pair a week.

Time passed and the classes were ending. Bob asked me if I'd like to come by the park after I finished teaching that Saturday and see the final testing for the dogs to graduate. Shaunessy and I wandered over to the park and stood off to the side, as the various dogs went through their paces. Most, but not all, did well. Bob came over with Jake and explained to me what they'd been working on, and what was the final test. He said the dog must sit at your side at the command "heel." The instructor gives you a hard rubber ball, and you're to tell your dog to "stay." You are then supposed to throw the ball without the dog taking off, and then yell "okay, fetch," at which point the dog is to get the ball and bring it back. The advanced canine students were told to "halt" during their run for the ball, then were told to "sit" and then "okay, fetch" again. Only two of the remaining dogs passed the advanced behaviors.

As the last dog was returning with the ball in his mouth, Bob asked me if I thought Shaunessy could get through the test. I grinned and said I'd bet him five bucks he could. Bob had no way of knowing I'd been using the exact same commands with Shaunessy for a couple of years, only using a Frisbee instead of a ball. On the first try, the instructor gave us a ball, and we went to work. I took off Shaunessy's harness and told him to "heel," which he immediately did. I said sternly, "No fetch, you stay," repeated it three times, then threw the ball. Shaunessy didn't move a muscle until I yelled, "fetch." Then, he tore off like an NFL offensive tackle after a prime rib. I heard sounds of approval from the people around us. After only seconds, I yelled, "Shaunessy, halt! Sit! Sit, boy!" From the scattered applause I knew he'd done what I'd asked. Grinning from ear to ear I yelled, "Okay boy, fetch. Get it! Get it!" Again, I heard sounds of approval around me. "Did he get it, Bob? I asked.

"Yeah, he's got it in his mouth. He's about to bring it back."

Only a second later, I heard sounds of disappointment and "too bads" coming from the spectators as Bob leaned over and said, "Hey Roy, it's a bummer, but you owe me five bucks. He just dropped the ball on the ground and trotted off to the hedge near the edge of the grass."

"Damn!" I muttered half aloud, "he was almost home free."

Suddenly everyone started laughing and Bob slapped me on the back. "Well man, I owe you the Abe."

"What do you mean?" I asked. "I thought you said he dropped it."

"Yeah, he did. But he just went over to the hedge to take a leak, then ran back to the ball, and here he comes with it now!"

55. She sings great, but Man— What a Dog!

As the years passed, old Shaunessy got too arthritic and brittle to get up and out to work every day. I'm sure a few of us have had the same feelings at one time or another as we get a little more ripened and mature. Ever notice how much more difficult it is to decant yourself from a low-slung sports car or speedboat than when you were a younger, more "crisp and supple" vintage?

My old boy was still the boss at home, but my new guide "Liesha" had to take over his daily guide duties. Often over a short beer, I know as if I could see him, Shaunessy would come over to me and sit, looking up with his soulful brown eyes. I could visualize his hat askew, his worn teeth stained and yellow from hand rubbed Cavendish pipe tobacco. The thoughts were racing through his old devious dog persona, "Hey man, she might be a good lookin' young blond, but she sure as heck can't get total strangers to talk to your blind butt nearly as well as I could!" If he could talk, I'm sure he was right on. I've had three dogs after him, and though each was fabulous and special in their own way, none of them ever demanded the attention Shaunessy brought to us. He was like a canine magnet.

Liesha was a sweet, good-natured golden Labrador. Like so many of her breed, if a burglar broke in the house, she'd show him where all the good stuff was— for a biscuit of course. Once, when she heard one of those air-compressor starters fire up on a transit bus, she backed straight out of her harness and split the scene, heading for the nearby "bun and run" opting for a hot dog, leaving me holding an empty harness. I secretly hoped someone would say, "Hey dude, you lost your dog," just so I could say, "Oh no, my man, I just found this great harness." I know compared to other guide dogs, my Liesha wasn't the brightest lantern in the storm, but she saved my tush many times, and I loved her dearly. I've always challenged myself with teaching my dogs little tricks and behaviors for others' and my own amusement. But Liesha didn't take to most of them as well as others. Her claim to fame was her ability to bark on command, especially when I sang to the kids at school. She'd come over and sit next to me, and when I said, "Liesha, speak," she'd chime in with two barks almost perfectly on the beat. The favorite of the kids, especially the young ones, was the tune "If You're Happy and You Know It." I'd play the guitar and sing, "If you're happy and you know it, Liesha, speak." "Bark, bark," she'd answer. The kids loved her, of course.

One morning the students from a local elementary school came to our school for an exchange program, complete with their own classroom music. We'd all gathered in the theater for the youngsters' presentation, and the teachers from the other school were videotaping their students interacting with ours. As luck would have it, their last song was, you guessed it! As soon as they sang the first line, they were joined by a canine alto from the back row. No matter how I tried to squelch her outbursts, every time they reached the place in the song where the kids did the call and response, Liesha barked twice: "If you're happy and you know it, clap your hands, BARK, BARK!" Our visiting students didn't make it through their song, for most began to laugh at Liesha's spirited participation, and most of the audience was imitating her barking.

People on the whole seem to love dogs, and even those who don't are usually intrigued with guide dogs. I have fielded some of the wildest questions by folks on buses, trains and even airplanes. "Do you sleep with the dog?" one young lady asked me once. I fibbed a bit and said, "Well ma'am I used to. But she snores much too loudly, and it disturbs my dreams." Something happens at least two or three times a week. I can be sitting on a train, or in a store shopping, when someone will invariably come up to us and start talking to my dog, carrying on a monologue for minutes. During that time, they totally ignore me as if I didn't exist. They often preface the monologue with, "Oh, look at the pretty blind dog. Are you working hard today? I bet you're really tired," etc. Sometimes I have to chomp on my tongue to stop from making dog grunts in answer to their questions. More than once I have been a wise ass. It's always fun when a young (or not-so-young) lady asks my dog, "Hello, gorgeous baby, how are you today?" I can't help it. I have to say, "I couldn't be better, perhaps we could do lunch."

I have an extensive collection of guide dog jokes and cartoons people have given me over the years, and some I've had enlarged and laminated to hang on my walls at school so the kids with some vision can see them. One of my favorites is hanging on my classroom door. I'm told it shows a large German shepherd sitting next to a pretty female French poodle. Her toenails are painted, her eyelashes are long, and she has a diamond necklace instead of a collar. In the background is a blind guy dressed in a suit and tie waiting at a crosswalk. The dog's harness is hanging from his left hand, draped over a fire hydrant. The shepherd is saying to the poodle, "Well, baby, I guess I'd better get back before he figures out that light can't possibly be that long."

You have to tell this next one with a southern drawl. Three "good old boys" are sitting on the porch of the feed store. One turns to the guy next to him and says, "Sid, do you know my dang dog's so smart, I can give him fifty cents and he can go down to the store and bring me back a copy of the 'Livestock News.'"

Sid says, "Shucks, Joe Bob, that Ain't so smart. My hound can take a fiver from me, go down to that store, pick up a six-pack o' beer, bring it back, open a can, and drop the change from his mouth right in my hand."

Joe Bob turns to the third fellow on the end who's blind and says, "How 'bout you, Gaither. Your guide dog that smart?"

"Well," Gaither drawls slowly, "I don't rightly know how smart he is, but he owns that store."

I lost Liesha to a relatively rare canine liver disease when she was only six. Her loss was tough to take. A few months later, I found myself with a bright and sensitive black Labrador, "Cricket." I know of my four guide dogs, she was the most cunning and strong-willed. Most everyone who's ever had a dog thinks theirs is brighter or more unique than the one next door, but Cricket truly was an exceptional animal.

After I first got her, my wife and I bought one of those large insulated plastic igloos, made especially for large dogs. It had a built-in floor and looked exactly like its name. The tunnel-like entrance jutted out perhaps sixteen inches from the rest of the structure. We brought it home in the back of a pickup, and as I unloaded the thing, I sang my version of an old song, something like, "He Ain't heavy, he's just bulky." It was definitely a "bring your lunch" deal!

I finally wrestled that Dog-loo into the back yard, intending for Cricket to stay in it only during the rainy weather when she was outside. I was soon in for a rude awakening. She wouldn't go near the darn thing. I tried every trick and gimmick I could come up with to get her to go inside that blasted igloo. I put pieces of my clothing inside it. In retrospect, perhaps even for Cricket, the dirty socks weren't such a great idea. She had a small rug she always carried around the house we called "the boyfriend," but as much as she loved it, she wouldn't go inside to get it. I even got down on my hands and knees and crawled inside the damned thing, trying to coax her inside. Bombed! My wife said she'd give a million bucks for some of my students and colleagues at school to see me peeking out from inside that fool thing.

Finally, one night I came up with what I thought was a brilliant idea. I'd tried putting food inside long before, but with no success. I knew she loved bones, so voila! After dinner that night, I boogied outside with some beef rib bones, her favorites. I took a three-foot throw rug for her to sleep on and placed it far inside the igloo. Then, I piled the bones near the back of the rug. My wife Jan said after I stood up, crossed my arms and said, "Get the bones, Cricket!" the dog looked up at me like I was nuts, then turned and stuck her head inside the opening of the igloo. "She's going inside!" Jan said excitedly. I'm sure a large grin came over my grill as I realized that the superior intellect of man had again triumphed over the inferior intellectual gifts of the animal world. Cricket bent her head, grabbed the border of the rug in her mouth, and backed out, pulling the bones on the rug outside. I heard "crunch, crunch" and she was gone with her treasures. Thankfully, the store gave me a complete refund on my Arctic brainstorm!

One of the biggest problems with not being able to see is not knowing who or what is close by, who's listening, and who's not. Once, while standing on the train platform with another teacher from the C.S.B., I was carrying on an animated conversation about something or other and Cricket was not at all impressed with my diatribe. She kept rubbing against my leg and whimpering, grumbling for attention, feeling quite ignored. As my friend spoke, I turned and said, "Sit!" She immediately obeyed. Only a minute later, as I began speaking again, she returned to her same bratty behavior, clearly jealous of my talking with the other person. Again, I said, "Sit, baby!" I'd just opened my mouth to finish a sentence when she again was up whimpering and rubbing her head against my knee. A little exasperated this time, I spoke loudly, "Darn it baby, for the last time, I said sit down and stay!" Only seconds later, I heard my companion trying to stifle a laugh. I thought at the time his reaction seemed a little odd under the circumstances. Later when we'd boarded the train that'd pulled in, he leaned over and whispered, "Roy, there was a nice, young oriental woman who was standing just on the other side of Cricket. After you told the dog to sit so firmly the last time, the poor woman's eyes got really big. Then, she turned around, rushed over to the seats on the platform, and did just what she'd been told!" Hey, Big Mouth, have a little face on your egg!

56. Close Encounters of the Absurd Kind

It's good to know I'm not the only guy with some challenges to have a sense of humor. One afternoon after finishing teaching, I was walking in the pouring rain with Cricket toward the train station. The home stall and feedbag were wafting their irresistible call. Cricket was plodding along at her steady pace, and I was reliving my early life as a barnstorming, decorated fighter pilot, taking giggling, voluptuous farm girls for joy rides in my Stearman biplane (or perhaps how much my damned feet hurt from standing most of the day). Suddenly up ahead, I hear the sound of a small dog yapping and a strange whirring noise. As we continued walking, I recognized the whirring was the sound of an electric wheelchair. I then assumed the person in the chair had dogs with them, so I told Cricket to move to the wet and muddy area beside the walkway, allowing whoever was ahead to pass with no obstruction. As the person in the chair came closer, I was surprised by a gruff and not very friendly voice speaking loudly, almost indignantly, "What's the matter, you blind?" My mind raced for a second, for I was a little miffed since out of courtesy I'd just moved out of the way for this person.

I blurted, "Well, yes sir, I am. How 'bout you, you really short?" Only a few seconds passed, and the man began laughing, and I did the same. In only moments, we became a couple of idiots stopped in the pouring rain talking amiably about our dogs.

57. Give Me a Brick to Build a Dream On

Cricket loved an area in the finished basement in our house near my exercise equipment. She'd often sleep there at night. A friend at school had to move and give up his Shepherd pet and gave me a large dog pillow for "Her Nibs." It was thick and nearly square, and she quickly took it as her own.

One evening, an hour or so after I'd let her out for the last time that night, we went upstairs to hang up the day. Minutes later, we heard a strange scraping sound coming from downstairs, then silence. Perhaps ten minutes, later we heard it again. Hoping supernatural creatures hadn't decided to visit and party with Cricket in the wine cellar, we went down to the basement to see what the source of the noise was. Jan started laughing soon after turning on the lights. We'd only recently finished having the basement remodeled, and a pile of common building bricks had been left stacked in the corner near the furnace opening. Cricket had, one by one, slid the bricks across the floor and made an irregular border around her pillow with the bricks. I couldn't believe it until I felt them with my own hands. They weren't perfectly lined up, but close enough to see what she had in mind. The frosting on the cake was that no more than a week after I replaced the bricks on the small stack, she rebuilt her crib again! I thought of having a small sign made for the wall above where she slept, "Current Architect and Resident, Francis Lloyd Lab."

Often when I play somewhere and I'm recognized, they'll ask me, "Where's your guide dog?" I stopped taking her with me years ago for mainly one reason. I know in the same situation I'd probably do the same, but often as I'm trying to play music, folks play with, talk to, and try to feed the dog. For over ten years, I played music in a large and popular French restaurant near Mission San Jose, in the south bay area. There were three dining rooms in the place, and I'd sit and play in all three at least twice a night. In the two largest rooms I had a small table next to me where I kept a tip jar, some business cards, and an occasional glass of vino, shared with me by the boss or a steady customer. Cricket always lay on the floor under the table, out of the way of passing customers. With the tablecloth above her, in the dim light, she'd often go unnoticed.

One evening I was singing a request for the "Theme from the Titanic" for at least the fourth time, when I knew something was amiss. Cricket was fidgeting around, and the bell on her collar was definitely clashing with my sinking ship noises. "No, Crick. Still, girl!", I mumbled between phrases. The ringing didn't stop, and if anything, got louder. Finally, and mercifully, my musical vessel slid below the surface. I moved my guitar over to my left leg and bent over far to the right, reaching under the tablecloth to calm my noisy beast. A couple, who just happened to be friends of ours, and steady patrons of the place, were sitting at the bar directly behind me. They saw the whole thing unfold. My hand immediately slid clear up between the legs of a formally dressed woman on her hands and knees under the table, where she was playing with my dog. In the noise of the busy night, I hadn't heard her soft voice. After replacing the table, cleaning up the wine, and sweeping up my broken tip jar, I can unashamedly admit I've been "under the table" once or twice in my life, but not with such embarrassing results!

58. Have a great trip! See you in the fall!

I've talked with friends many times in past years and have learned of numerous instances where their guide dogs had saved them from disaster. Cricket gave me more than one of the same. Often during lunch hour, I'd take her on long walks to the local shopping center a mile or so from the school. I knew it was good for her to walk unfamiliar routes, so we often returned a different way than we'd come. One day, I picked a particularly meandering route and almost made the evening newscast. We'd gone around a large man-made lake in Fremont and started back in the direction of the school, past the new police department and city buildings being built along our route. We reached an area where the sidewalk was blocked, and Cricket took me off the sidewalk along the curb in the concrete gutter of the wide, but busy street. A city employee working nearby yelled to tell me the sidewalk was blocked off for nearly three blocks ahead. I thanked him and wrestled with whether to go back a quarter mile and try to cross the street to the opposite side at the last intersection or continue the way we were going. I knew Cricket was great at obstacles, so I decided to continue. She was unbelievable. At every storm drain grate we passed, she led me around it, and I remember at one point we had to go around a vehicle of some sort parked along the normally "no-parking" curb. I remember thinking at the time there seemed to be an unusual number of storm drain grates along the stretch. We walked for what seemed a very long time, and I knew by now the sidewalk must be clear. I told Cricket to "get the sidewalk," but she refused to move to the right from the gutter. I guessed we'd not yet reached the end of the construction zone, so I continued to follow her assured lead. We walked another hundred yards or so, and I knew we'd long since passed the three blocks the man had described.

171

Again, I gave her the same command. As before, she refused to move to the right toward where the sidewalk should be. I decided to step up on the curb and test with my foot to see if the sidewalk was still blocked, or clear for foot traffic. She fought me, resisting my direction. I should have known instantly something was very wrong. Holding her harness handle in my left hand, I stepped up on the curb and put my foot out to feel for the two-foot wide median of grass, that normally ran between the curb and sidewalk for over a mile in that part of the city. I knew it was there from our going that way some months earlier. I felt her pulling on the harness with rigidity in her body. My foot dropped down into thin air. There was nothing there!

It seemed an eternity as I teetered on one foot in midair before she pulled me back. I know to this day that had I not been holding her harness handle firmly, I'd have fallen in face first. Suddenly, at that same moment, she pulled me further back and a voice screamed from far below the level where we were standing. "No! Don't step that way! Someone will be there in a second! For Christ's sake don't move!"

I jerked back shaken and confused, for I hadn't heard any strange noises, but the voice was coming from an odd angle, and it didn't make sense. I heard footsteps running toward us from up the street. Soon a concerned voice boomed, "That was close, man. You almost had it!"

"What's happening?" I asked, still not understanding the situation. The man put his big hand on my shoulder and led us forward, the way we'd been going earlier along the curb. As we walked, he said, "Right off the curb to your right, where you stepped up, is nearly a four-story drop. It's almost straight down. We're digging down for the basement floors, security cells, and power and communications bays for the new police station. The sidewalk isn't there anymore. Once we finish the walls and foundation for the basement floors, the sidewalk and landscaping will be refilled and replaced. I'm really sorry. You stepped up on the curb area right in between the barricades. Your dog was taking you past them and going in the right direction. It's only another hundred feet or so and the sidewalk is back to normal. Do you want me to take you the rest of the way?"

A little choked up and shaky, I said I thought we could make it okay. I thanked him for his help and felt the tears well up in my eyes as we walked the next hundred feet of the curb. In a smooth and practiced motion, Cricket slowed, then turned in front of me, letting me know to turn. As she stopped, I felt with my toe and again found the curb. Beyond it was the grass and sidewalk I'd expected earlier. We turned left, and she began walking on in her normal cadence, as though we were starting from home in the morning. I told her to halt and squatted next to her. By now the tears were running freely down my face as I hugged her, holding her head close to me for a very long time. I knew then and will always accept: Love and trust are two things we should never question or refuse.

59. Waiting for Mr. Lee

"Come on, baby, give me a little sugar." The old man's voice always sounded as gentle as the patter of warm summer rain. Every weekday late afternoon while I waited for Jan to pick me up, I'd hear the gentle old African American's same friendly words, spoken softly through the din and bustle of the Fruitvale BART station. Then, as always, the next few moments would be filled with his warm voice talking to Cricket. "Have you been working hard? I bet you're ready to go home 'bout now. Give old Lee those soft ears."

Owners of dog guides are taught to tell others not to pet the dog while they're working in harness. But from the first time Mr. Lee appeared, I couldn't make the words come out of my mouth. So, each day as he bent to stroke my old girl's head, I always listened to his conversation as if it were the first time I'd heard his words. Our topics often varied, but there was always the weather, and how his wife was working too hard now that he was retired. On some days, his wife's train would be late, and he was really sorry he had to leave his small fifteen-year-old terrier in the car while he was talking to me, but he said his aging little buddy had a definite attitude around other dogs. Often as he watched for my wife's car to appear, Mr. Lee would continue talking to me as noisy trains and traffic passed by, and I often didn't hear more than a few of his soft words. This pattern continued for at least two years, and no matter how aggravating or dismal the daily news seemed to be, he never changed his gentle and philosophical approach to the fast-paced life around him. Every day our conversation would begin as if no time had passed between our last words. I'd be a liar if I didn't admit that on a few days (usually one of those that had been intense at work), when he'd stroll up and start talking, I would have preferred to continue listening to the jazz on my CD player or daydream about what might be in store at home for that evening. But even on those rare afternoons, when his voice wasn't as welcome as usual, in seconds we were back on comfortable and soothing ground.

I haven't seen Mr. Lee for nearly a year now, so I don't know what has become of him or his family. I want to be optimistic and think that he comes at a different time than before. I certainly don't want to dwell on any other reason for his absence. I do know rarely a day goes by that I don't find myself listening, half expecting to hear that same gentle age-wizened voice.

His absence has brought some heavy thoughts to mind. I truly believe that there is an untapped treasure of knowledge and information resting dormant in the still agile minds of so many of our senior citizens. It's a damn shame there aren't better ways for our young Americans to reach out and assimilate some of those priceless skills and information embodied in our older generations. So much, so soon, will be lost forever. Sadly, we need to be reminded that there is a wonderful treasure in the dignity and warmth of the elderly, perhaps a sense of caring and openness of days past. Whenever I think about Mr. Lee, a worn but very real saying crosses my mind: We don't really know how much we appreciate someone who comes into our lives until they are no longer with us. I lost Cricket and Mr. Lee in the same year.

60. I Almost Got the Point

The feelings a blind person experiences shortly after a near accident or mishap are difficult to describe. I'm convinced they're not exactly the same as those of a sighted person. I'm not in any way downplaying the fear experienced by the sighted in any given situation, but the blind don't have the benefit of a series of visual cues before, during, and after the incident, allowing them to make instant corrections. It's more like an instantaneous realization, hitting you like a square-point shovel on the side of the head.

Some years back, while walking briskly with my new dog guide, Oliver (believe me, Oliver did everything briskly), excuse the cliché, I experienced a real eye opener. One of the pitfalls of having a good guide dog is that you can fall into a sense of security and complacency once the dog is familiar with the route routinely traveled. I think I was daydreaming about something I was going to teach in one of my classes that day (or possibly, what did my wife put in my lunch today?). In any event I'll admit I wasn't paying much attention to our progress down the street. Some new condominiums were being built in an area that only months before were gladiola fields. Oliver suddenly jerked to a stop and wouldn't budge. Immediately I began searching the sidewalk in front of us for any obstacles, fallen branches, shopping carts, or broken places in the surface of the sidewalk. I felt nothing. I held up my hand and swept the area in front of my head, to see if a hanging branch or bush was jutting out in front of my face. Nothing was there. I thought perhaps something was in the way a bit farther ahead and maybe he could go around it. "Pass, boy, pass," I said, but he wouldn't move. Slowly I inched forward as he continued to balk, feeling instinctively ahead with my foot, and in front of my face. What I soon felt made a sickening sensation run through my insides, making me grit my teeth thinking of the consequences if Ollie hadn't stopped when he did. In the next few minutes, I learned that a large truck carrying construction materials for the builders had been parked at a slight angle in the same direction as the sidewalk, covering all of its surface and extending into the street. On carrier racks, mounted high along the top sides of the truck, was a collection of twelve-foot long lengths of rebar. They're the metal rods used in concrete pads and walls of buildings to strengthen the concrete when it is poured and formed. The rough, sharp end of one of the half-inch in diameter bars was pointing directly at my face at eye level, only inches away! I don't want to think of what my skull would have looked like if we had walked into that metal spear at full speed. I suppose a six-foot shish kabob. No thank you, not today! A certain young black Labrador received a more than ample portion of dog treats from my stash when we reached the school later that morning.

61. The Torch of Life Burns On

For over twenty years, I've had the good fortune to have a lasting contact with the Pac Bell Pioneers, a wonderful group of retired telephone employees. They were responsible for developing the game of Beep Baseball for the blind. A few months before the Summer Olympic Games in Los Angeles, I received a call from one of their members. She asked if I'd be interested in running the Olympic torch as their representative. Make my month! I was ecstatic, a little nervous, but very honored. It was a far more moving experience than I can describe. At first you don't think too much about it. It's something very special, but you're just running down a street with a burning thing held up in the air. "Sure, buddy!" I say.

I think that next to the birth of my son and daughter, it was the most exhilarating feeling in my life. If you could mix all the emotions you can imagine unity, patriotism, and pride in your fellow man and country— you've about scratched the surface. I have to admit, much to many of my liberal musician and teaching colleagues' dismay, I've become a staunch conservative and bit of a patriotic nut. But I've traveled for years and am convinced we've got it all right here at home, more than we'll ever realize. So, you can see, having been a slime-sucking recruit, with my die-hard flag waving mentality, I was a perfect candidate for the torch gig.

I can't lie. I had frequent nightmares, and in my mind's eye I saw the newscast lead line. "Flash, CNN: Blind runner misses turn and extinguishes eternal Olympic flame in San Francisco Bay." Once, after sharing my feelings about the pride I felt while carrying the torch, and later hearing about folks lining the street and waving our flag, one of my colleagues at work said,

"What about those people from all over the world taking part in the Olympics? Are they less important than our country, or you or me?" Aren't the participants supposed to be 'all as one?'" Of course, in concept her statement couldn't be more right-on, but there was clearly something more inferred beneath the surface of what she asked. The question torqued my jaw, for it reeked of the misguided mentality that has slowly permeated our society, something about not outwardly showing or admitting pride in the excellence and values of our country.

Knowing the woman who'd asked the question was in earnest, I replied, "Those from other nations feel pride and love for their land and birthplace, and many have much less tolerant governments than ours, yet they aren't ashamed or too P.C. to wave their flag with honor and pride." Man! I just twisted my ankle trying to put that sunscreen on the back of my neck while getting off my soapbox. It's an unbelievable coincidence, but of the hundreds of thousands of miles the torch had traveled, my route carrying it took me right past the music store I once owned! Each runner was to run the torch for one kilometer, and at that time the running outfit and torch were given as a gift to the runner after the flame was passed along to the torch of the next participant. Of course, the presentation was given after removing the togs in a nearby changing area, certainly not in the buff before your applauding fans!

As I started out with two sighted runners next to me, I felt my heart nearly pounding out of my chest. The event was being in all the local newspapers and television stations. In truth, the only way I'd have received any more coverage was if I had been arrested driving a Formula 1 race car in the nude, with a ten-foot cane out the cockpit. I smile at my embarrassment and appreciation of all the attention. Without a doubt, I know if a blind guy was going to be running something on fire down the middle of my street, even if it was just a beer drinking seatbelt, I wouldn't want to miss it, just to see how the whole thing turned out.

The first hundred yards are a complete blur in my memory, but I remember the tall, older-sounding runner to my right yelling that there were helicopters above, and motorcycle police escorting us front and back, along with the television vans. It didn't take long before my right arm began to feel like I was holding a Sumo wrestler above my head. I switched the torch to my left hand, not realizing how many dozens of times the motion would be repeated before the run was over. At that time, the torches weighed over three pounds and were filled with propellant, with a wicker and wick-like center at the top. After about a half mile, I knew the greatest problem wouldn't be my fitness or lack of it, it would be the fumes from the jet turbines of the helicopters and the exhaust of the vehicles around us, along with the smoke from the torch itself. But I felt as if I was two feet off the ground, and looking back now, I don't know if it was due to the exhilaration of the moment, or the effects of the fumes. The chop of the helicopters' rotors above and their screaming turbines made it impossible to hear much of the crowd noise along the way, but occasionally I was given a boost by the sound of cheering. Every so often, people along the street would run out and shake my free hand, and many times women would run along beside and kiss me (Hey, this has definite possibilities!). You know, now that I think about it, I assumed they were all women.

The kilometer passed by so quickly that I barely had time to feel the impact of the moment. Then, the runner next to me, who'd been giving me directions and never did seem to breathe hard, informed me that we were about to stop and pass the torch to the next runner. It was near the San Lorenzo Village, no more than a hundred yards from the site of Shaunessy's hostile take-over of the post office jeep! I was breathing pretty hard, more from the adrenaline rush than from fatigue as I'd been jogging for the last few years at regular intervals. I knew I wasn't ready for fifteen rounds with the champ but had felt I was in good shape. You can imagine my surprise when soon after we stopped, and people began to gather around, the man asked me, "Do you think you can run it another leg? The young lady newscaster who was to take the flame from you has suddenly become very sick to her stomach and isn't able to run."

"Sure," I blurted, not even thinking of what I'd just agreed to. I slammed down a couple of small glasses of Gatorade and was on my way again, pounding down the street. He said our next pickup point was at Kennedy Park, next to the Hayward Airport. "Piece a cake," I said to myself, as my lungs continued to burn from the exhaust fumes. But I was so proud and jacked at that point, I could have had an IV needle in my arm and been pulling the hanging bottle on its caster stand alongside of me if necessary. For one of the few times in my life, I felt like Paul Bunyan in a bulletproof vest.

The crowds were even larger now. I could hear them clearly above the noise of the vehicles around us, and I felt the hand of the man next to me on my shoulder as he yelled to me to slow down. "Ah! My prayers are answered." In truth, I was already going at a less than Olympic pace. Compared to some poor crawly critter, I was flying. I guess it's all relative. My running companion shouted, "There's a guy jogging up on your left, probably to shake your hand."

Seconds later, a beefy mitt gripped mine and the stranger yelled, "My name's Rick. You used to teach me guitar at your store years ago. I've got three kids now and no hair."

The last section of the second leg has completely faded from memory, because my tank had suddenly hit empty. I think it was a combination of weighing over two hundred pounds and the adrenalin wearing off that left me sounding like a wheezing steam locomotive. I do remember standing on the lawn of Kennedy Park with crowds of people around me, bending over, still trying to get my breath. Sweat dripped off my chin and nose, falling on my worn running shoes. I tried valiantly to sign the pieces of paper given to me for my autograph. I had a tough time; my hands were shaking so badly. A reporter from the local TV station was urging me to come with her to give an interview, but at that moment I couldn't have moved, even if my wife had offered me a bottle of Cabernet and a steak.

Every few Olympics, I pull out the torch and show it to the new kids at school, and once in a while, I'll pass it around among friends at the house. It's a great conversation starter, and on the Fourth of July it's a gas to use it to light fireworks. Darn it, I still love to wave that flag.

62. Found

I had no warning that the summer I ran the Olympic torch would be the changing point of my life. For as long as I could remember, shadows from the past taunted me. Every birthday was filled with unasked questions never getting answers. Floyd and Anne never gave me straight replies to the things I would ask on rare occasions, questions about how I became part of the family. Eventually, I just resolved to force myself to only think of the future. Still, those vague memories persisted, shadows of something I had once experienced. Often, I'd wake up in the night, then question the silence if I'd ever hear the answers to my gnawing feelings about my past. I was sure of one thing. Inside was an emptiness, an unexplainable void, in spite of their assurances I was their adopted son. For years, I felt strangely alone and cheated after overhearing Floyd's rare drunken outburst, about me not being his, and the chances he was taking with the law. Yet, at times I was torn by deep guilt. Over the years, they'd fed and clothed me. Could they understand or accept my inner turmoil? Would they think that I was just selfish and thankless? Why didn't they share the truth? After decades of those vague memories, even after Floyd and Anne's death, my past was still a mystery. One balmy day just following the Summer Olympic Games, all my questions were mercifully answered.

I leaned back on the couch in my front room, my mind still reeling from the shock of an unbelievable discovery of that afternoon. Slowly, I tried to make sense of the words I'd just heard on the phone only hours ago from an older sister I never knew existed. Taking a swallow from a glass of red wine, I leaned forward and tried to visualize what she must look like. Was she dark-haired? Was she tall or short? What color were her eyes? What had she thought that night a week ago, when she watched a close-up of the strangely familiar face move across the television screen during an evening newscast? The face was so haunting, etched with by years and the adrenalin rush of carrying aloft the Olympic torch. The muscular man was running past the flashing cameras of newsmen and spectators in California. Suddenly the blind runner's face had an identity. She'd memorized the worn photos of her two-and-a-half-year-old brother, having searched for him so many years. He'd been taken from her and her mother so long ago. She turned to her husband who had tolerated her searching for decades and said, "I know you think I'm crazy Sam, but that man looks just like my baby brother Wayne!"

As it had been many times in past decades, the telephone again became her strongest ally. Having become a master of search, she was soon excited to find that the runner's unfamiliar last name matched a new name that she'd found only weeks before hidden in some dusty letters from a deceased relative's treasures. While still a child, she'd sworn to our mother that someday she'd find the little boy they'd loved and protected. Six-year-old Barbara Lee was too young to comprehend the reasons why someone would want to steal her brother away. But true to her promise, she'd never stopped looking. Now, with this new name she'd discovered, she worried as this new search began. After nearly thirty years of letters, calls, and inquiries, was she finally near an answer? Or was this just another bleak and gut-wrenching dead end?

Only hours earlier that afternoon, I'd thought, "Who could be calling me long distance?" Troubled, I heard my shoes crunch the dead leaves and twigs on the sidewalk as I hurried from my music classroom toward the administration office of the School for the Blind to answer the call. I was so preoccupied with my curiosity that memory guided the way. My white cane became just an unconscious extension of my body. The hair on the back of my neck tingled, as I listened to the warm, drawling voice on the line. "Now Roy Wayne, don't y'all hang up that phone. This is your sister, Barbara Lee, in Tulsa, Oklahoma." My mind fumbled for some reason or thread of recognition. My first thought was the caller was just jerking me around. She's one of my adult students at the local music store, or one of the customers or employees from the nearby club where I was playing guitar and singing. Then, a chill of uncertainty and disbelief crawled through me as the warm voice said, "I know bubba. You got thick dark brown hair, hazel eyes, and a birthmark behind your left knee. I've got a picture of you and me when you were two and a half years old. Mom had it taken at a photo studio, and you were wearing a knit suit with knee pants and a short-billed cap. Baby, you were stolen from Mama and me by our stepdad, Leonard, up in Washington State. He was only married to her a few months when he deserted Mama and the army during the war. He took you 'cause he probably knew the MP's wouldn't bother him if he was dressed in civilian clothes and had a young child with him. Many years ago, with the help of the FBI, Mama and I found out he'd left you with some migrant workers down in the cotton fields in Arizona. It took us days to drive there, and then we found we'd just missed you by hours. Food scraps were still on the table in the tent house where you'd been staying. The migrants had moved on. Someone said they thought they saw you go away with a young couple in a black Ford, and there the trail ended. I just figured out days ago, the folks in the car were the people that raised you. The wife in the car was the sister of the man who kidnapped you. They took you from the farm workers because she couldn't have children. After we just missed you, that was when Mama broke down. Her mind and body just couldn't take any more. She got so sick; she was in the hospital for nearly all the next year. But I promised her I'd never give up looking for you." Numbed by the impact of my sister's words, I couldn't speak. I felt like I'd been shoved into a blast furnace. I began perspiring freely, and the breath seemed to have been sucked from the depths of my lungs. Her voice sounded so distant and surreal, and yet so strangely warm and peaceful. It rang through once again with a mixture of emotions I'll never forget: "BUBBA, MY BABY BUBBA, I'VE FINALLY FOUND YOU. MY GOOD LORD, I'VE FINALLY FOUND YOU!"

I know I would do anything possible to take away the pain and despair Mama and Sis must have endured for so many years after I was taken from them, but I know there's nothing remaining to do but to put into perspective the events following that day. I realize much of what I am today and my outlook at this moment is a direct reflection on those events, along that winding path from the past. I'm sure you' will agree, in many ways, life and the way we grow and change is a mystery in itself. It's taken me over a decade and many prayers to forgive Floyd and Anne for the terrible thing they did to my mother and sister, and to me for that matter, and may God rest their souls, for I know the inner turmoil they must've felt daily as they were constantly looking over their shoulders for the law. I'm sure they knew the consequences of their actions. I know now why they couldn't tell me the truth, yet I will never totally understand their motivation to bring such pain to Mom and Sis, for we know now that through the years, they knew exactly where Mom and Sis were living, even after Mom remarried. Still, my understanding and their constant guilt can never soften the anguish and loss caused by their actions. It may sound odd, but I have to thank Anne and Floyd for giving me the best they could, in their own misguided way. I truly believe that over the years, they convinced themselves that in some twisted way, they'd done nothing wrong.

Only weeks later, after Sis's call at the school, I met my birth mother for the first time in over forty years. It seemed impossible, but for years she'd been living only a two-hour drive from the Bay Area, in the foothills of the Sierras southeast of Sacramento. I vaguely remember talking to her on the phone and getting directions to her home in Mokulmne Hills but was so nervous I don't have a clue what was discussed. When we drove up, she was waiting outside in the driveway, her husband of the last thirty years, John Bass, at her side. We hugged for a very long time and cried a great deal more, then went inside. We spent a few days together, then I had to get back to work. John said after I left, Mom slept for nearly eighteen straight hours. The story is bizarre, but with all the craziness in the world during wartime, not totally unique. My mother Alice's first husband, Clifford, whom she'd married in Oklahoma at the age of sixteen, was my sister Barbara's father. After my sister was born, Cliff and Mom split up, and Mom and eighteen-month-old Sis came out to California. Four years later Mom fell in love with my birth father, Jack, but after I was born, he wouldn't marry her. For whatever reasons, Jack left us all behind in the Central Valley of Southern California to drive supply trucks near the end of the war. The following year, Alice met a tall, good-looking soldier named Bill. He said he was in security work in the military. Alice gave my sister many photos of him in different uniforms, with various rank markings. After he went AWOL from the army, Alice found out that his real name was Leonard, and that everything about him except his last name was a monumental collection of lies.

Leonard Chandler was the consummate con man. One afternoon while Alice was at work, he came by the house and told the babysitter and my sister that he was taking me to a doctor's appointment on the military base. That was the last they saw of me for nearly four decades! Alice and "Bill" (Leonard) had only been married a few months, and we found out years later, he'd been married over seven times, often to more than one woman at the same time! One of my points of closure of this tangled mess, besides being reunited with Mom, is that the creep's been dead for ten years now.

Anne Mae Siligo, Floyd's wife (now also deceased), was Leonard's sister. Leonard called Anne and Floyd (the couple in the black Ford in Arizona), who at the time were living in North Dakota. Leonard called them from Arizona, and said he had trouble with the law and had left me with some very distant relatives, migrant cotton harvesters who were now working the fields. He lied to Anne, telling her my mother had been abusing me badly, and he'd taken me away for my safety. Now, he said he couldn't take care of me anymore and was asking if she would come down and get me, and that he'd help her out financially later. Of course, he never did help her out, but I ended up staying with Floyd and Anne from that point on. After Anne's death, her only living relative (a younger brother) told me she could never have children and desperately wanted them. Anne had known my mom, Alice, before I was taken. She was the one who gave me my first haircut when I was only a year and a half old, held in my mother Alice's arms. Now, I've had the time to see everything in perspective, and my negative feelings, felt for so many years, have been tempered with time and love. So many children around this Earth have suffered and fought to live under the harshest of conditions, so how could I ever feel mistreated or unfortunate? The experience of working with and teaching those much less fortunate has reversed and obliterated any bitterness remaining. Life is too precious and awesome to waste a second on negative memories or "what-ifs." The sad fact is that those around me, who were part of the events of my upbringing, were affected from the guilt and injustice of their actions far more deeply than myself. I feel such love and closeness to my sister, so blessed to have been finally found by her, and then be reunited with my mom through sis's efforts. Until mom's death in 2004, I talked to her every day, and spent quality time with her every chance I could. Up to her last days, her mind was as sharp as David Letterman's tongue. Nearly every time we would get together, I made recordings of her singing timeless Irish and Early American folk songs, as she played the dulcimer for us while I accompanied her on guitar. Her husband John, a true navy hero, is buried next to her, but his priceless stories and factual accounts of many U.S. naval battles and operations over his thirty years of service have enriched my life so much. I truly hope the memorial for American WWII veterans in Washington is visited by millions. For John, a gifted and proud man, like so many of his era deserves, the lasting recognition for his service and dedication to future freedom for all of us.

We don't always realize how much the truth impacts us and our new directions in the future, but one thing is sure: as tenuous as modern life is, knowledge is a strong weapon in the battle with uncertainty. Modernists say the truth is what we want it to be, but perhaps it's something similar to a gift waiting to be opened. We might love it, or we might want to return it the next day. Either way, we're richer for the experience of learning the truth. Every morning as I listen to the sounds of each coming day, I say a prayer for the Lord to watch my newfound family, and others who are or may have been lost, as well.

Only a few weeks after my sister found me, I received two round-trip airline tickets to Oklahoma from her husband, and my wife and I flew there as soon as we could. I was ecstatic and scared spitless to meet Barbara, my new-found sister. She was just as she had sounded over the phone, a shapely, cuddly woman with a sharp wit and quick mind and emotions ready to be revealed at any moment. Over the coming years, I saw how much Babs had in common with our mother. At the Tulsa airport, I met her bigger-than life husband, Sam. He alone had financed her years of searching for me. Picture as I did, a six-foot-tall barrel-chested farm lad, who through his own drive and hard work, had made it big-time in the construction business. Sam wore the finest boots (selected from his collection of dozens of the same,) a Stetson when the spirit hit him, tailored jeans, and western shirts. He sported a couple of large diamond rings and had a laugh that echoed off far walls. A man no one messed with, but most everyone for miles in any direction, not only respected but either loved or disliked in envy. Sam and Babs owned most of the property of the little town of downtown Mounds, a half hour South of Tulsa, and lived in a stately refurbished old mansion built by an early oil baron. Nearly anyone who had kids or was having a tough time and needed a short loan only had to come to Sam, but dear Lord, they had better pay it back! I spent a fabulous week with them, and the following description took place at a museum a few hours' drive from Tulsa where many famous Remington sculptures are on display.

63. Get Your Hands Off That Woman! She's Busted!

We arrived in the early afternoon, and after passing through the entrance, Sam paid for the tickets for all of us as I protested loudly, "God, Sam! I'm not flat broke, ya know. It's not right that you pay for everything."

"My treat, Dinkus!" Sam laughed. "Your first trip to Oklahoma." Sam spoke to a woman behind a counter. He asked, "Excuse me ma'am, I have a question?" When she answered that she'd be glad to help, I heard that her southern accent was beautiful and high-pitched, and I was instantly reminded of a pretty young girl I'd known next to a lake many years earlier. "My brother-in-law here is totally blind, he's from California, and he's a damned good musician, and loves art. It's his first time in Oklahoma. Is there anything inside the museum he can touch and feel what it looks like?" I noticed the woman's silence for a minute. I thought maybe that question had never been directed to her before.

"Well, sir, the rules specifically say that no one is to touch any of the displays—that's the curator's rule. But I'm the lead day director, and I believe, in this case, we can certainly make some exceptions. Perhaps we can call it an extension of sooner courtesy. Of course, you must promise to wear these." I heard the sound of a drawer opening. "Here are some flannel gloves. We use them to move the displays so as not to leave any oil from our hands on the surface of the exhibits. Please wear these at all times and return them when you leave. Sir, only touch the large stationary objects—statuary and metal work would be best. I must insist that you not touch anything that's canvas or linen and, of course, anything behind glass."

"Killer! Sam blurted. This is gonna be fun. Come on, Bubba, let's soak up some culture."
I felt Sam's strong hand on my arm as he pulled me back toward the center of the corridor like I
was his little brother. "Here, put these on." I pulled on the gloves, then took back my cane I'd
given him. Years ago, I discovered that walking with friends sighted guide, I rarely needed it.
Almost as if Sam had read my mind, he said, "Roy Wayne, open that cane. That way people
won't freak out when they see ya touchin' things, or maybe they'll just think you're a
professional pool player." Grinning, I flipped the elastic band off the end of the folding cane, and
it sprang out to a five-foot length. Tapping it softly on the polished floor, I knew from the sound,
the floor must be wide tile or marble. The sound of the cane echoed as we passed the first two
passageways leading off the main corridor.

"Where we headed, Sam?"

"Bubba, I love bronzes. It's the first thing I want to check out. Remember that American
sculptor Remington? On a business trip a few years ago, I went through a private collection of
some corporate mogul in New Orleans. He's got dozens of Remington's bronzes like these on
display, big things, some of 'em four feet taller than me. All kinds of animals, Indians riding
horses, I'm tellin' ya, Bubba, they looked almost alive." We made a right-hand turn down one of
the corridors, and I noticed as the sound instantly changed; I heard the ceiling was lower. "Here
they are, man, look at that! Baby check out that one...some kind of cat. Can't be a lion— doesn't
have a mane. Hey, let me move this pole. It's connected to others with one of those velvet-
covered ropes, like they use in theaters; I'll slide it a few feet. Come on, Bubba, check this out."
Sam brought me to the small opening he'd made in the barrier and placed my hands where I
could touch the beautiful detail of the bronze cat. "That's it, you got it. It's taller than normal.
It's sittin' on a marble table about two feet high. Damn, in real life a cat that size would weigh at
least 450 pounds." Running my fingers along the tendons of the beautiful sculpture, I felt the
muscles in the back of its legs and smelled the pungent patina from the oxidation on the surface
of the bronze. The detail on the cat's legs and paws were magnificent.

"Come on, my man, there's a bunch more of 'em up ahead." For the next twenty minutes,
I explored and felt three more of the big sculptures on the right side of the corridor. Each time,
Sam carefully replaced the barriers back to their original positions. I was engrossed with
inspecting a bronze sculpture of a large work dog (as big as a St. Bernard) harnessed to a two-
wheel milk card, crockery jugs all inside, when I was suddenly jerked, my hands pulled away

from the cool surface of the metal as a booming voice shouted from behind me Startled herself, I heard Babs gasp as the man roared in Slavic accented English, "Can't you read the signs we have posted? You will notice they are in English and Spanish. It reads you're not to touch the exhibits at any time. This rule is strictly enforced!"

Sam had turned toward the burley guard and described him to me later. The man was in his middle thirties, perhaps thirty pounds overweight. His uniform was from a thinner year, and his neck veins protruded while his mustache twitched with each word. As he sucked in his breath his face glowed red and angry. Sam said he thought, "Damn, this old son takes his job seriously." I slowly backed away from the statue as Sam gestured to Babs to explain. She said, "I'm sorry, sir, but the Day Director of the museum gave us permission to touch the statues, and these gloves. My brother is from California and is blind. He may never be able to come here again in his lifetime. We wanted him to feel some of your beautiful artwork, since he can't see it."

The big man spoke back firmly, "I do not care where he is from, or anything about your brother's vision. I've been given a responsibility and my instructions are clear. If you wish to remain inside the museum, you must abide by the same rules as everyone else. If I am forced to warn you again, you will be escorted to the exit. Do you understand completely?" Sam said the man's legs were wide apart, his fists on his hips—as he stood defiantly.

"Certainly, officer, your orders are clearly understood." Sam spoke sarcastically. He grabbed me by the arm, "Come on, Bubba, let's beat feet outta here before Generalissimo Franco back there guns us down for insubordination."

I felt a mixture of emotions: embarrassment, disappointment, and was a little hurt as I said, "He's hardnosed, Sam, but we have to understand, those are the rules and he's just doing his job." We moved on into the next gallery. Intermittently, I tapped my cane, listening to the intricate echoes from the spacious, high-ceiling galleries. Babs and Sam kept a running narrative of the displays on both sides of the walkway.

"Baby, come on," Babs said. "On this side of the room, there are tapestries that go back to the Byzantine era, and some before that. On the far left, there's a collection of rare Pakistani and Indian weaves. It's amazing. The colors are still brilliant!" She continued, "Many of the elegant villas throughout Spain have these tapestries hanging on the walls, like we do with portraits or paintings in America. They're particularly prized in the hunting lodges and homes of Spanish nobility, and I as understand, they're always hung—rarely do you find one on the floor." I knew from the sound we'd moved through an archway into another gallery, but it had the same high ceiling.

"The lighting's softer in here, Bubba," Sam said. I heard the shuffling and clicking of shoes all around us. I knew there must be hundreds of visitors close by. A few children chattered in curiosity, and I heard a wide variety of different languages. "Bubba, most of the lighting in here's indirect. They've got special spotlights on some of the bronzes and larger pieces, like in that first room we were in. It highlights the shadows and lines of detail. The paintings are on fabric, and they don't want any direct light on them. It ruins the pigments."

We turned once again into a smaller corridor with a lower ceiling. Sam whistled softly, and Babs explained, "God, this is gorgeous marble statuary, Bubba—here's cherubs, warriors, and some sacred pieces. The one off to the right looks a lot like the Pieta at St. Peters in Rome. I saw it in a book a couple of years ago."

"Ahh, man! Look at that one." Sam moved quickly across the corridor to the left, dragging me behind him. As we stopped, Sam said to Babs, "Look around behind us, see if the badge man is around."

"No, Sam, I don't see him, but the lighting is not very good."

"Come on, Roy, ya gotta feel this." Again, I heard Sam move one of the metal stanchions. He grabbed my arm, pulling me toward the object that'd caught his attention. "Get this, man. It's about a nine-foot tall nude. She's layin' on her side with her head propped on her hand. She's layin' next to a pool, and sittin' on some rocks in the middle of it are two fish sittin' up on their tails. It's like they're talking to her. Here, bend over as far as you can."

I ran the flannel gloves over the cool surface of the marble where Sam had placed them, and soon I recognized a huge full breast, its nipple the size of a swollen wine cork. "Wow!" I blurted.

Sam ran my hand down the long curve of the woman's side and up and over the tapering swell of her full hip, then down the muscles of her upper thigh. It seemed to me, from her hip to her knee was at least four feet.

"No!" came the booming voice from behind us.

"Busted," Sam exclaimed almost gleefully.

The guard was breathing heavily as he rushed up to us. Sam had already replaced the metal stanchion holding the rope. The guard's speech was clipped and fast, "Immediately, you will leave from the main entrance. You were warned, out now!"

I'm sorry, I knew I'd broken his rules, and we had been warned, but at the time, his over reacted anger sounded comical and out of place. Sam said the guard took up a position behind us as we moved back toward the entrance. Sam leaned over to me, "It's okay, my man. You got to feel the finest lookin' thing in this whole damn joint."

"Left—here," the guard spoke tersely. Babs took my arm softly as we began to turn. Suddenly, Sam jerked to a stop as I felt my sister do the same. I heard a strange thumping sound, then an immediate rippling of agitated conversation around the corridors nearby.

"The house lights just went out," Sam exclaimed loudly. "I mean, Bubba, its pitch black in here. I can't see a damned thing."

"What do you mean?" I asked. Aren't there any windows anywhere or skylights?"

"Remember this is a museum. They don't want any sunlight in here. I mean...I tell ya, man, it's like bein' inside a bank vault."

I heard the beginnings of whimpering cries from frightened children, then soon, the calming voices of their mothers urging them to be silent. "Aye, mites, how do we get outta here?" I heard someone speaking with an obvious Australian accent, only a few feet away. I heard a clatter of racket as someone knocked over a metal stand or signpost. I heard the guard cursing emphatically behind me, trying to operate his electronic communicator in the dark. The guard began to push his way past us towards the corridor ahead. There was another loud crash as he collided with something. Minutes passed and as the power remained off, the conversation around became more anxious and animated. I turned to Sam, "Well, Mr. Barrett, I believe this is my chance to do something useful. I tipped my head back and yelled, "Please, everyone, quiet. Please listen to me. If you will follow my voice, I know the way out. Everyone come to the sound of my voice, carefully. I'll lead you to the main entrance of the museum. Please, keep your hands out in front of you and move slowly." We soon heard the sound of shuffling feet and quiet whispers as people began to move in our direction. "Here, this way. We're walking toward the doors now. Follow the sound of my cane."

I began tapping loudly and walking toward the end of the gallery. I heard people shuffling behind us. I began to hear larger numbers of others coming from the adjoining corridors. I turned left, retracing our path leading to the main corridor of the museum. I'd remembered exactly how long this gallery was for the echo from the ceiling had intrigued me when we'd first passed through an hour before. The crowd behind me now was nearly silent. Only the sound of their shuffling feet and soft whispers came from behind. Soon, I heard that the echo of the cane was becoming more pronounced and knew the main corridor was just up ahead. The clicking reverberation off the marble and concrete walls changed abruptly as we entered the main hall, and I immediately turned to the left.

"There—up ahead," Sam spoke. "Bubba, it's somebody with a flashlight. There are those wooden doors we came through after we paid for the tickets. Hey, Dinkus, you're amazing."

Seconds after, Babs said, "There, I see light. They're opening the doors right now."

"Yeah" I agreed, "I hear the street beyond." Many voices cheered from behind us, and we heard multiple sighs of relief as the other visitors saw the light up ahead.

"Escape from the Bastille!" I grinned and shouted. Soon we'd passed through the high hardwood door of the entrance. Sam returned the gloves to the lady, and I acknowledged a few thank you's from folks as they passed by. We stood off to the side as couples and large groups moved past us toward the street. Everyone was talking with animation and relief. At least five minutes later, the last one to leave just happened to be the burley guard.

Sam saw the look of disdain on his face. "Roy Wayne, Generalissimo is standing right behind you, man! He's pissed."

Oh yeah? I couldn't resist the chance to get in a quip. The chain of events had offered an opportunity I couldn't pass up. I used my cane and took a few steps in the guard's direction, then spoke with mock sternness, "The next time I'm here, it might be wise not to yell at me so rudely, and you shouldn't be so nasty to my friends. If you don't sweeten up, When I make the lights go out next time, you'll have to find your damn way out all by yourself!" As we walked forward, Sam laughed from his belly and took Bab's arm as she smiled at the guard. There was no question of his anger as he launched a few choice curses in my general direction. I knew no blind guys from California or anywhere else for that matter would be at the top of his next year's holiday greeting card list!

64. Okay coach, how do you do it?

There are millions of people around the world who are losing their vision slowly and even more who are related to someone is experiencing this predicament. In the following section, I'll give a few of the techniques and adaptations useful in daily living with vision loss, and this will answer a few of the many questions people have concerning how someone gets along when they can't see. You might want to share this information with someone who is experiencing progressive vision loss.

Since the alphabet begins with A, that's the first letter of the two most important words to all who have to live and deal with a disability: **ATTITUDE** and **ADAPTABILITY**.

Attitude can help you enjoy one hundred percent of your daily life. A very bright blind student of mine once showed me this formula:

If you write out the twenty-six letters of the alphabet and write numbers under each letter (A Is number one, B is number two, C is number three etc.) every word in our language will have a numerical value. So, the word Attitude has the following number sequence: A is one, T is twenty twice, I is nine, T again is twenty, U is twenty-one, D is four, and E is five.

When these numbers are added up together, they total a perfect one hundred. Just for fun, try adding up the sequences of some other larger words and see just how unique the word attitude really is.

ADAPTABILITY is one of the greatest gifts of being human. We can adapt our behavior to fit a transitional situation and, in some instances, we can even change our environment if need be, to fit our needs or wants. For those who are losing their sight, it is very natural to first have a very desperate fear of what is going to happen to them in the future. Will they be able to do the same things they did when they could see well? Will they suddenly be enveloped in a dark world no one else really understands? Will people treat them differently because they can't see? These and a thousand other questions cross our minds and haunt us until at some point we learn to deal with them and finally mercifully put them to rest. A comment made to me a few years ago by a taxi driver in Germany still rings in my mind. After questioning me about my dog guide and vision problem, he said, "I don't know how you do it; I think if I lost my sight I'd have to die!" I told him he would more than likely do what everyone else does when something just as traumatic happens; you "keep on truckin'" and work around the challenge. You may not like it, but somehow, the strength of the human spirit along with some help from others will get you over the initial shock and help you learn to adapt.

It's only my opinion, but I have always believed that people who lose their sight later in life have some advantages over someone born blind in conceptual and informational processes, but have a much tougher emotional time accepting their blindness and having to deal with that major change to their lives. However, there is one small advantage to losing your vision slowly. You are given time to adjust to the process and find other ways to accomplish everyday tasks and routines, and, of course, the most valuable asset is the fact that you have memory of what things looked like before your vision loss.

Please understand, IN NO WAY am I suggesting the individual born blind at birth is any less functional or capable, only that it is necessary for them to assimilate information and visual concepts by other means than a person who at one time had sight. Over many years, I've noticed that those blind from birth are far more accepting and comfortable with their disability and often don't think of their vision loss as a loss, only an aggravating annoyance at times. The once sighted person often remembers colors, what clouds look like, the multi-hued streaks in the magic of a sunset, or the beautifully curved and flawless symmetry of a running stallion, or the grace of the dancing human body. The toughest challenge is to the elderly person who loses their sight to diabetic retinopathy or macular degeneration, for they have lived nearly all their lives in the sighted world.

Th fact is, we are now living much longer that we would have in past decades due to the wonderful medical advances we now enjoy. Because of our new life longevity, doctors are now seeing a larger percentage of the population with latent vision loss. Often, and much quicker than we might think, the aging people find themselves in the terrifying throes of an approaching speckled, snowy world of no or very little visual information. Most sighted folks think what a blind person sees is just darkness, and in some cases, this is true; however, in most cases, the visually impaired individual sees a slowly deteriorating blurred image of mixed information. This is somewhat the same as years ago when you would see the snowy image when you changed channels on your TV. Try imagining the between-channels' "snow" on the screen super imposed over a normal image with darkened, less distinct areas and you have a general idea of the image a person with retinal degeneration sees. Of course, without getting technical, there are dozens of other forms of blindness, some having nothing at all to do with damage or defects in the eye structure but having its cause in the optic nerve or visual cortex of the brain. This can be caused by a myriad of reasons, i.e.: trauma to the brain, hereditary anomalies, etc.

In some limited cases, the progressive loss of vision can be slowed or treated to a degree by micro-surgery and changes in lifestyle and diet; however, in most situations, the degenerative process continues at varying rates. "What a downer thought," you might think, but simply put, it's dealing with a reality. Unlike so many folks around the world, here in the good old USA, we have some great options and adaptive technologies available to us, to help our quality of life. We can all rest assured that with the newer research on stem cells, artificial visual receptors, and microsurgery and regeneration, many currently blind young folks will one day be able to see in the future.

Vision may not be through the usual way we think of vision at present, but perhaps a bypass of the neuro pathways to the visual cortex by computer enhanced soft and hardware. I am not going to be tedious by giving list after list of web-sites and organizations that benefit the visually impaired, but quickly, here are a few organizations that can help you, or someone you know, get help in learning to live with vision loss in their daily lives: NFB, the National Federation for the Blind, AFB, the American Foundation for the Blind , and the venerable but fantastic resource in Louisville Kentucky, APH, the American Printing House for the blind and visually impaired.

This last resource has thousands of large print and Braille self-help materials, as well as thousands of aids and technologies to make your life easier as you deal with diminishing vision.

The greatest problem arises after we have come to grips with the reality that we are truly losing our sight. Every one of us who experiences this trauma goes through a series of steps of denial, anger, a certain amount of self- pity— the "why me" syndrome; but eventually we realize, 'Hey, I have to do something about this mess!" Sadly, the "deal with it" scenario doesn't happen overnight, and instead, usually in small incremental steps.

Mobility instruction is the first big stride. You have to keep moving and work at keeping your independence, routine, and movement around your daily tasks. There are orientation and mobility instructors that can be engaged from rehabilitation services. These wonderful teachers can help you learn to use an extensive list of products and techniques to help you get around. The first thing people think of for mobility for the visually impaired is the white long cane, but even before this great tool is needed or required, there are many other aids that can be introduced right away: a monocular for reading bus displays and street signs, magnifiers and specially designed lighting and viewing tools for use at home, even specially designed eye wear and filters for your particular vision problem

One of the first things most people notice when their vision starts to fail is the lack of acuity in dim lighting. There are many aids that can help, but sometimes in rare situations, even a small flashlight can't be of much use, as shown in this true story.

One evening, a fellow without great vision took this foxy young lady out to dinner at his favorite fancy restaurant. About halfway through the meal, he found he had to use the men's room. He excused himself and retreated to the back and returned in only a few minutes. As he continued his conversation with the comely miss, he kept noticing a draft. To his great embarrassment, as he set his wine glass down and replaced his napkin in his lap, he felt that his fly was still open. Carefully and discreetly, as he gazed around the room, he reached down and zipped the offending apparatus up and continued with dinner.

At the end of the magnificent meal, after the bill was paid, he jumped to his feet to help the young woman with her chair. She jumped up a second later and backed away from the table, a look of total shock on her face. As he rushed toward her, to his disbelief, he realized he'd zipped the tablecloth in his fly. At that point of realization, he couldn't stop quickly enough and pulled the cloth and the entire contents on it off onto the tiled floor. Imagine, after the hellatious crash, standing in the middle of a dining room with a tablecloth hanging from your fly, trying to explain to a gorgeous woman how it got there!

After mobility issues, reading and accessing information is the next, and most important, skill to address and adapt. Low vision specialists, often available in university clinics and larger health vision plans have a wealth of devices, lenses, and special apparatuses to help you magnify or accent the printed word. Nearly all modern computers have a screen magnifying program, (Zoom Text, etc.), and of course, when your vision deteriorates to the point where you can no longer read a computer screen, there are marvelous screen reading programs that can help you access the internet and most all major publicly accessible sites. These programs allow you to navigate the information on the screen and type material into the computer, all while reading the information back to you in a pleasant and very understandable synthesized voice.

I'm using JAWS from Freedom Scientific this very moment; it's one of the best screen reader programs available at this writing. As with all technologies, no one product is perfect, but they all are constantly being upgraded and are able to access more and more information every day. Many are not aware that there are easy to use scanners that utilize OCR or Optical Character Recognition to read documents and materials and transposing them again to synthetic speech.

65. The Big Question: Large Print or Braille?

What I'm about to discuss is probably the most volatile and touchy subject identified with loss of vision. Put in simple words, many individuals with poor vision don't want to use Braille for they feel it has the stigma of labeling them "Blind." They feel that as long as they continue to use large print and magnification, they are just folks with "poor" vision.

I know what I'm talking about, for because for years I was one of these same people. Gradually, I found that I was reading less and less, especially newspapers and novels, while shying away from watching television. I was avoiding reading menus in restaurants, and not even cooking as much as I liked, because I couldn't read the darned recipe books and food containers. The small handheld magnifier I'd used for years was no longer cutting it. Without realizing it, I began listening to more and more recorded books and materials, and even joined the Library of Congress talking book program. But something was missing, something I missed very much: independence.

I don't remember the exact time I started learning Braille, but it was, at first, a slow and laborious process. Had I had a teacher in the beginning, I'm sure it would have been much easier, for there are some techniques that really do help you learn to read the raised dots on the page. Fortunately for me, a colleague at CSB took me in tow and showed me some simple concepts as to how the system of dot writing works, and I promptly learned it in one summer.

I have had sighted students in public school that have learned grade one Braille in only an afternoon. Grade one, simply explained, is the alphabet with a few punctuation marks. Notes to yourself, short recipes, phone numbers, and addresses can be written with the Perkins Braille writer, a type of Braille typewriter. Of course, with the fabulous increase in technological innovation, at present, there are many electronic devices and Braille computers, with a Braille keyboard and refreshable dots that pop up on the display, which allow you to feel what you've written. Once one learns grade one, grade two is a natural step. It uses contractions and full word signs, a sort of Braille shorthand. For many low-vision individuals, a knowledge of grade one is plenty. Using a Braille dimo-labler, you can label anything, from green tea containers to CD's and DVD cases.

One morning, while riding to work on BART, a guy across the car from me announced, "Hey man, you've started a new dress fad. That's really fresh, one black shoe and one tan." On a recent trip back East, I'd purchased two new pair of loafers on sale. They were identical except for the color.

Of course, I was embarrassed, but quickly replied, "Right you are my man, and I'm so happenin', I've got another pair just like them at home!" Soon after my fashion statement, I began Braille labeling on the bottom of the soles on all my pairs of shoes, placing the tiny plastic dimo-label on the sole next to the heel. "Br" is brown, "Bl," pf course, is black. And if "M" is mauve, then "P" must be puce. Remember, I live near San Francisco and more exotic footwear is sometimes needed for some gigs! One should never lap-dance in black shoes.

I believe something very deeply and think a lot of folks' hang-ups about things would be eliminated if they followed this simple rule: "Forget about what you think other people think. If doing something out of the ordinary helps you, do what works for you." If you know someone who's losing their sight please tell them, "don't be afraid of learning Braille, even if you just use it to label and identify things, you will find it's a marvelous tool." Also, there's a wonderful piece of technology that came on the scene not many years ago, the digital recorder. I personally prefer the Olympus personal digital recorder. This little helper fits in your pocket and can be used to record notes to yourself, phone numbers and addresses, and even directions to destinations you can use along the way. They hold a ton of information and can be downloaded to your computer. It is easy to use by the visually impaired once you become familiar with its individual features.

Probably the most useful tool on the scene now is our smart phones. Each new season, it seems, some new feature or app is featured on the variety of phones available. We can record, edit, and use them for a myriad of tasks. I recently asked one of my students why he wasn't wearing his Braille watch anymore. He answered; "Why wear something on your wrist that only does one thing!" Often as we get older, we are less open to newer technologies and techniques. We must try not to fall into this trap, for the new things we learn will open dozens of doors to new and exciting paths. I'll close this section on information access with another true story.

Soon after I learned to read Braille, I was riding on another bus with a Braille book open on my lap. I was reading slowly, both from lack of experience reading braille in a moving vehicle and because of the calluses on my fingertips from playing fretted instruments. I remember the book very well; it was on the history of jazz. The bus was quite full, but I had forgotten about anything else around me as I was completely engrossed in the marvelous story and the wealth of information I was reading. After some minutes had passed, a sweet lady sitting across from me got up to get off the bus.

"Are you alright young man?" Her voice startled me out of my reading.

A little confused, I asked, "Were you speaking to me?"

Why yes, I was," she answered softly. "I was concerned if you were okay, because for the last few minutes I noticed you have tears on your face."

I didn't know what to say for a second, and after I wiped my cheek, the words tumbled out. When in doubt, tell the truth. "Yes ma'am, I didn't realize it, but I guess I must have been crying, but it was from joy. I've just learned how to read again."

66. Always Try Something New!

In this next section, I want to share some information and tips about and revolving around one of the joys of each day. I know food is not at the top of some folks list of daily pleasures, but I know for a fact it certainly is to many and no matter how dedicated we might be to our work and other daily tasks and hobbies, we still have to eat at some point. No matter how convenient, we can't eat pizza and hamburgers three meals a day forever.

When eating out or at home, those losing their sight have to go through another of those Twilight Zone periods where they're neither fish nor fowl. The first thing we must learn is don't be afraid or embarrassed to ask for help, whether you are in a store or a restaurant. Oddly, the reason many totally blind customers shy away from asking for help in restaurants is because servers often want to give too much assistance. All of us, no matter how poor our vision, want to have independence and to feel at least somewhat in control, so it's a tightrope as to when to bring it up that you no longer need someone's assistance. I found years ago, after requesting an elbow to follow a server to a table or booth, a simple smile and a "Thank you so much for your help, I can handle it from here, you've been really helpful!" makes things smoother. This gives closure to the situation and in no way embarrasses the helper or the folks who might be around you at the time. The first rule of dining when you don't see so well is discovery. Now, this is not as earth-shaking as entering a newly opened Phoenician tomb or climbing through the caves of a lost extinct volcano but does involve some simple detective work. Once you're seated, make a gentle search of the items on the table near you, starting from the borders and working in. It doesn't take a rocket surgeon to know you have to be careful not to overturn any tall or slender objects on the table. These tall objects on the surface of a cloth covered table are the visually impaired person's worst enemy. On a varnished or waxed surface, they will often slide or move when bumped, but on cloth— timber! I think my wife and I have spent thousands of dollars over the years purchasing squat, heavy containers, glassware and the like, that when placed on the table, are not easily knocked over when bumped. Just remember, even those with twenty-fifteen vision have knocked over wine and water glasses in the finest restaurants.

The next task is organization. Don't be afraid to move things around, place your drinking glasses and napkin where they are most useful to you, and then do the same with your silverware. When I'm in a nice place with semi or formal table set-up, I usually put my wine glass in the center above my plate and the water off to the right. When reaching for things, there is less of a chance of spilling something directly in front of your plate than if it's placed off to the side.

ALWAYS, when you pick an item up off the table surface, lift it straight up for at least ten inches or so before bringing it towards you or wherever you want to move it. Then use your other hand to clear the area where your about to replace the item (of course, you don't have to clear the area of your mouth!). Keep all of your plates, salad and main dish, near the front edge of the table, but not off the edge. Believe it or not, because you are not reaching so far to gather things off your plate, there is a smaller chance of spilling things on the table in front of you. There are many techniques that are invaluable when eating out or at home for that matter, so don't fall in the old ditch of always eating things that are familiar and that can be eaten easily or with your fingers. By doing this, you slam the door to some marvelous new taste treats and dining experiences. As your sight diminishes, at least twice a month, ask a companion or spouse to go to a new and preferably different ethnic cuisine than the food you're eat on a regular basis. It's a stimulating and challenging break in the routine and makes you use some of your newfound eating skills. Don't be afraid to ask your server questions about the new place's food. Nearly all servers and cooks are flattered when you are curious about what they serve.

When in a restaurant or coffee shop, I always ask for my salad to be placed in a bowl instead of a plate. It's so much easier to get the chopped veggies and leafy contents on a fork and not be continually pushing it back to keep it from going on the tablecloth. Having the salad in the bowl also mixes the dressing continually as you eat. Of course, when dining out, you can cut your own meat and large vegetables, but be sure to get a sharp knife from the server. If the knife is unusually large, you must refrain from spontaneous Samurai impersonations. But remember, most cooks and chefs are more than happy to cut your entrée while it's still safe in the kitchen. All that's required is for you to ask.

If you are right-handed, as you eat, every few bites use your left hand to rotate your plate counterclockwise. Always approach the food with your right hand from the outside edge of the plate moving toward the center. As the plate turns, this simple technique will help keep the food away from the edges of the plate and will not push it off the opposite side. When eating off plates and salad bowls, ALWAYS keep a small piece of roll or bread in your free hand. This will allow you to push mobile food and pickled octopus onto your fork or spoon with ease, and also help keep the food centered on your plate. I've been told that in a warped humor since, there are few things more frustrating or amusing to a sighted observer, then watching a blind person chase a cherry tomato around a large salad plate, often approaching speeds of an Indy 500 racecar. I have found it's much easier to bite the bullet (or tomato in this case) and use a spoon to capture the elusive spheroids. Other folks around the table can easily be temporarily blinded by the flying juice from one of the slick critters finally being captured and speared with a fork. ALWAYS put a napkin, cloth or paper, in your lap. Thus, vagrant portions of cherry tomato or pickled octopus will come to rest there and not on your bare feet, designer cut-offs, or tank-top!

Another important word and practice is **CONSISTENCY**. Get in the habit of arranging the table in the same way wherever you go, whether it's Burger King or a five-star French cafe. It becomes second nature to reach for familiar items without having to search the area around your space. I learned the hard way. Be careful to always have your silver arranged the way you want it and off to the side, out of the way of glasses or other items you might be replacing on the table in front of you. Here's another true fiasco of mine. It happened when I was still trying to fool the world into thinking I could see.

This took place in a very posh little place in Carmel, California named the "French Poodle." I was being interviewed by the ex-wife of a very famous rock star; she was now a local entertainment agent, and I was as nervous as a banjo picker at Covent Garden. The lighting was very dim, and the tables were small, and of course, I couldn't see the menu. I overheard the couple at the next table say how darling it was the menu was handwritten in French. I dodged the menu bullet by saying I didn't read French. I know the lady I was with was dressed exquisitely because of the compliments from the Maitre'd.

I wasn't aware at the time, but it happened that my agent acquaintance was fond of vintage brandy, and for her sake, I'm thankful she had ordered us an ample serving before my soon to be center-stage act. We had an appetizer and salad, and I was doing quite well, despite the fact that except for a few candles, I could barely see a thing in the dining room. Maureen, my dining companion, decided to order a bottle of French white wine. For the success of our future business dealings, I had no idea white wine would be a blessing in disguise. We were drinking our second large glass after an exquisite meal, when I reached forward and placed my glass on the crowded table. Somehow, in all my scarfing of the great food, my silverware had been moved around and I had forgotten that earlier in the dinner I had pushed a utensil away with my water glass. What happened then would be nearly impossible to recreate, but the handle of the fork I hadn't yet used had been turned away from me, and when I set down my nearly full glass of wine (I must admit, it's rare I set down a nearly full glass of wine), I must have placed the bottom of the glass right on the edge of the handle of the fork. I was in the middle of a demonstrative description of some great artistic triumph or perhaps my recent formula 1 victory at Monaco, when I bent forward to emphasize my words. Opening my hands for effect, I bent toward her and placed both elbows on the table. To my disbelief and horror, my right elbow came down on the tines of the offending fork and flipped the handle up in the air. Of course, the wine glass that I'd placed on the end of the handle became airborne and, before shattering in a hundred pieces, must have flipped in the air above the table, dumping most of its contents on the face and upper body of my surprised and soon vino soaked companion. I was amazed she took the entire mess with remarkable poise and good humor, remarking how I had a true gift of bringing attention to myself in any situation. I'm not sure that was a compliment. After she dropped me off at my hotel, because of her fragrant condition (her dress had a marvelous bouquet, with crisp berry nose, and fruity esters), I worried that she would be stopped on the way home that night, and I had no idea of the location of the nearest bail bondsman.

Maureen proved to be as good as her word, and for the next year and a half, I spent a blurring mass of weeks and months meeting recording producers, aging stars, and a few of my true idols. We had lunches and dinners with dozens of entertainers and talent brokers. I was confident, maybe even a little cocky, knew I could sing and play guitar well, and was fortunate to be decent looking, but my timing for bursting onto the music scene was lousy. To my own demise, at that time in my career, I didn't have enough sellable original material, so I experienced one door slam after another, and soon had a very jaded opinion of the commercial talent and music business.

When I leaped off the carnival ride near the end of the next year, I was able to salvage most of my sanity, but nearly had to check into an alcohol rehab site. Still, when I think back on those crazy times, the experiences taught me so much, about myself, dealing with the gut checks of reality, and gave me an appreciation and understanding for the insecurity of others. Despite the disappointment and frustration of the experiences, I was able to be a part of some exciting and near borderline fantasies. I have to admit, I'm still glad that on that night at the Poodle, Maureen didn't order red wine!

Here are a few more tips you might pass on to a friend losing vision. Salt and pepper shakers are easy to distinguish. Smell, of course, is a good indication of which is which, but it might look a little strange for you to be sniffing salt and pepper shakers at Petite Maison Ristorante Francaise. If you pick up matched salt and pepper containers, the saltshaker is nearly always the heavier of the two. Of course, in fancier diners, servers usually dispense fresh ground pepper. Even in fast-food places, sugar packets are always heavier and shake louder than sugar substitutes, and nearly all shake on sauces have a distinctive cap and bottle shape.

Hot liquids can be a problem, especially if you are in a noisy restaurant or coffee shop where someone is serving you. Before drinking, always hold your coffee or hot drink, under your nose for a second to feel the heat arising from the liquid. Countless times, visually impaired patrons have had their mouths scalded by a cup of coffee they thought was half-filled but was just recently topped off by and efficient and silent server. Pouring liquids from larger containers is always a little dicey but touching the inside rim of the glass or cup receiving the re-fill under, and just behind the pour spout area of the pitcher or larger container allows less chance of spillage. Here's another trick for use at home I thought of years ago. Anytime you need to fill a smaller cup or glass with liquid from a larger pot or cardboard container (half-gallon milk cartons or large plastic juice bottles are a good example), move the smaller container to the edge of a sink, and then lower the larger one so its bottom is in the sink below the level of the counter. This allows a better angle to pour the liquid from the larger container, especially if it is full. An old but workable trick is to place your fingertip over the edge of the glass and pour until the liquid touches the fingertip. This method is not recommended for pouring melted lead into molds for cannon balls or testing the thickness of molten gold for your bullion bricks collection! I have learned to gauge the general fullness of a glass of iced tea or soda, by the sound of a fingernail tapping on a spoon resting in the glass. Another sure-fire indication you've more than filled your flaming Incan Coffee, is the overall decibels of the screams around you as you ignite your Men's Warehouse tuxedo. But one sure method if you're not alone is to ask your companion to fill the darned glass in the first place.

Here's another winner even some sighted folks may have experienced. When your tall drink with ice in it gets past half full, it's a good idea to occasionally stir the ice remaining in the bottom. It's really entertaining to all the folks at your table at the banquet when you tip up your glass to drink and the ice that has frozen together slides out of the glass along with the backed-up liquid behind it. Having no choice but to follow the rules of gravity, the clump of ice and liquid splatters down your chin to the front of your newly replaced Men's Warehouse tuxedo. Of course, after it melts instantly in your lap, when you stand, it looks like you've wet your pants.

Here's another tip that works well. If your resident eatery for the night serves fresh bread or rolls with dinner, it is much easier to butter it in this way. Often the butter or dried tomato, basil and pickled octopus spread, is served in an iced dish. It's more efficient to discreetly use a small teaspoon to dip a portion of this secret house treasure and then invert it over the edge of the roll using the rounded edge of the bread to scrape the spread from the spoon. You can then use a bread knife to smooth it over the surface if you desire. In not so fancy places, when the spread comes in covered pats, you can unwrap the little package and then apply it directly onto the bread while holding the still covered side of the square. Now if you think I'm certifiably nuts for dwelling on this, just keep your eyes closed and then try finding, then opening one of those little room temperature pats of butter with your nails and fingertips. Then, while holding the little pup, try finding a knife, and then scraping it off the foil and then spreading it on your still warm bagel-boogie delight. If you don't cheat and keep your eyes closed, I guarantee you'll be a candidate for a large bib, or a spot on "World's Funniest Videos."

Personal safety is always an issue no matter how well we see, but if you have, or know a person losing their sight, here are a few tips I've picked up over the years. Please remember, these are MY PERSONAL recommendations, and I'm not a mobility instructor, so at your own risk and danger for improving your quality of life, please do try these at home!

Your foundation is very important. I'm talking about your footwear. As strange as it might sound, as you lose the ability to drive your Ferrari, or ride with the gang on your Harley

Hog, you'll find that you're walking much more than when you drove. When you don't see well, you often will catch a heel, or stub your toes on objects on irregular surfaces and the occasional uneven curb or staircase can really be a literal pain. Except for dressing up for an evening function or a business meeting, wear sturdy comfortable shoes and your feet and hips will be as happy as a flat picker at a barbecue. For both men and women who wear pants, when possible always wear high thick socks (I often wear two pairs with the thinner on the outside). If you are a big walker or hiker, you'll never get blisters with the two pairs, and because they go up and cover a good deal of your calves, they offer great muscle support. When colliding with unseen obstacles the socks will also give some protection to the front surface of your shins. Do not however, expect the socks to protect you when kicking your best friend's rear to help them put their best foot forward. One common injury to those who have recently lost their sight is probably the most preventable. Ask those around you to observe this practice, (and learn to do the same yourself.) Never leave a cupboard door, drawer to a dishwasher, or inner closet door or entrance door to a room in the house half open. Even with your hands out in a protective position, you can walk into the door edge, often causing serious injury.

This next red flag is for anyone who is active in their community and attends more than the usual social function. Doors to building and room entrances are always to be respected. The following scenario can be nearly lethal to the person experiencing recent vision loss, and not yet using a cane. Find out as soon as possible where they're located, because sliding patio or courtyard doors are a silent trap, especially if they're very clean. It is not uncommon that a person with normal vision has walked through and shattered a glass partition. Once, when my vision was doing its "see you later" act, I was playing a union job at an exclusive golf course, I stood in line with the rest of the party and had a very elegant plate served to me, complete with prime rib and cheese baked potato. The band I was playing with that day did not know of my poor vision, and Dorkmaster Fuller here didn't have enough testicular fortitude to tell the guys in the band I needed a little help. Holding my pre-paid repast in both hands, I marched forward toward the pool area from inside the clubhouse with the determination of a stand-up comic opening to an empty house. I breathed easier as I saw the sun reflect off the pool outside and the people gathered around the tables but was suddenly hit with the solid realization, I'd just been run over by a beer truck! Of course, without knowing it, I had just walked into the closed glass door leading out to the pool patio. Sorry to say, my prime rib, potato, horseradish, and a good portion of my personal pride, ended up on the front of my tux, and lush carpet leading outside. Now it's quite possible the future ramifications would have been different if I'd been carrying tofu and broccoli, but I'm a quick learner. To make absolutely sure you don't walk through your patio doors or bathroom windows, at the risk of being arrested by the clean window police, you should never wash or clean them to where there is no evidence of something on the surface for safety's sake.

Those losing their sight must not forget, safety techniques are for everyone, we just have to fine tune some of them to fit our lifestyle. If you are not using a white cane, NEVER step into a darkened elevator without first touching the floor with your foot, and never walk through a dark square patch on the sidewalk assuming it's a shadow. A low-vision friend of mine once did this and stepped off into an open commercial terminal box in the sidewalk the power company had been working in. Some jerk had stolen the sawhorses equipped with flashing lights that had been placed around the hole. My friend suffered a broken collarbone and knocked out four of his upper teeth

There is one rule you must remember if you are losing your vision. Your memory of what things looked like in the past, will fool you into thinking you still see them the same way. Even if glasses do not correct your vision anymore, it's a good idea to wear them anyway. They will protect your eyes from branches, squirting cherry tomato juice, and other objects near your face during the day. When you bend down, always place a hand or both if possible, in front of your kissable visage. This will help keep objects protruding up from the floor from injuring your eyes and face. Of course, this little habit is not necessary, if for some reason, you desire to have your grill look similar to the cleat marks at the center of the Levi Stadium turf after a San Francisco 49ers game. But to be serious for at least a second, every day, doctors treat low-vision or blind individuals for facial abrasions and injuries, who were simply bending forward to pick up a dropped object from the floor in an unfamiliar area. Over time, and especially when not using a long cane, all of us who don't see well develop our own methods of using our hands to protect ourselves when we walk through unfamiliar or very dark areas. One of the most useful is the "protective arm position." The terminology of these mobility skills changes with time and area they're taught, but the techniques are simple. Try and keep your body weight forward on your feet so your balance is good, and then hold one hand up, palm away and fingers spread, in front of your face at nose level about twelve inches from your chin. Keep that same elbow out to the side at about shoulder level. Then, extend your other hand down in front of your waist. Keep the elbow nearly stiff and as you move forward, slowly sweep or "clear" the area in front of your body. Of course, at any time, you can stop and reach out with either hand for side tactile contact with walls or furniture. Utilizing these two points of reference and the sides and tips of your shoes (as well as the texture of the floor surface beneath your feet), after a little practice, you will soon be able to move quite safely and with amazing agility. However, naturally I wouldn't use these techniques walking down the central corridor at Macy's unless I was trying to do an imitation of Keith Richards the morning after the last gig of the Rolling Stone's "Steel Prostate World Tour.

Points of reference can make life much easier. Think of the large areas around you that you travel daily as a giant connect-the-dots puzzle. These familiar points can anchor your path between them. Most sighted folks think when you can't see, you must make physical contact with everything in your environment or you don't know what's around you. When your vision fails, it's not necessary for you to touch everything you once saw between the dots. You didn't touch them then, just saw them with your eyes. BY touching and making contact with walls, different textured surfaces and familiar non-movable objects, you can quickly learn to negotiate a large area. It's a well-known fact; those losing their sight quickly learn to use their ears to help feel the openings of doorways and even large objects in a room. I've proven this to friends for years. By utilizing sound and pressure changes, I can walk into a totally darkened room, having no idea of what's inside, and by feeling from the sound and proxemics of the reflection of sound in my ears, can move slowly through it without mishap. In a way that's difficult to explain, I can feel without touching, all objects above mid-thigh. It's more difficult to feel large things near the floor, but I can walk up to a wall and feel it in front of my face twelve or fourteen inches away. The term for this skill is called "frontal vision," but has nothing to do with sight. Over the years, I have seen dozens of students at my school that possessed this skill.

One great technique for travel in familiar areas is utilizing permanent shorelines. This doesn't mean quitting your gig and taking a month vacation to Aruba and sipping Mai Tais with your toes in the surf. It has to do with following the unique borders of traveling surfaces. (i.e., edges of sidewalks, borders of grass lawn areas, curbs and sloping driveway entrances.) Of course, it is much easier for the folks who have had vision, for they can picture these shorelines in their mind. But, by using the edge of your foot and walking carefully, you can negotiate long strips of street sidewalk or department store rugs. Even in your own house, memorizing the edges of your carpets and large area rugs can help you move quickly through a dark room. I have only a small amount of light perception in my left eye but have been known to walk all around my neighborhood without a cane, using only this shoreline method. I don't recommend you do it often, for you are much safer using a folding cane. Of course, while using the shorelines, you must be careful not to run over small children, smaller dogs, large visually impaired people using the shoreline method, or the occasional patrolling clean window policeman.

As you lose your sight, you don't have to give up your favorite forms of entertainment (except perhaps sky-writing love notes in your favorite biplane). There are countless web sites where you can download novels and transfer them to smart phone, Kindle readers, CD, or just listen to them on the computer itself, letting the screen reader read the text. Audible.com is my favorite site, but there are many others. Many books, magazines, and novels are professionally recorded and listening to them is truly "theater of the mind." The humble cassette tape is still readily available, and many free services will send you books on tape or digital recording once you are on their mailing list. "Books Aloud" in San Jose, California is my choice, but there are many across the country. Of course, there are many large-print books and periodicals available through the mail, and at your local library.

One fantastic newer innovation is the descriptive video. These are DVD or television digital video recordings that can be downloaded from service sites, showcasing your favorite movies and documentaries. They are beautifully done and as you watch whatever action you can on the screen (the newer high definition screens are magnificent for those losing some vision), an off-screen voice discreetly describes the physical setting and important action taking place on the screen. They are up to date, and even those with normal vision quickly adapt to the descriptive format. We should remember, most all public performance sites are aware of the need to serve the disabled, and they often have descriptive programs that accompany the action on stage.

If you are a sports fan, there are numerous companies that make some fantastic binocular glasses you can adjust for each eye and wear at any sports event. The field of vision is very good, and the players are brought right up in front of you. When you no longer have any usable vision, most inside venues have FM transmitters you can utilize to listen to the game inside, and of course, when outside, the old friend, the transistor radio with ear bugs can still be your trusty companion. One of the best radios I've found is sold by a great older company in Fortuna,

California. Their name is C Crane company and their earphones are magnificent for their low price and the small playing card deck size radio plays for days on just two AA batteries.

When you first begin using a folding cane, even if you're going to a game or crowded function with a friend, don't be embarrassed to take the cane with you. It's very useful on steps, aisles, and in the rest rooms. Also, the cane lets people in crowds know you don't see well. There is a dynamic that takes place while walking in public. When a sighted person approaches you in a crowded walkway, they assume you will naturally move slightly away from them as they pass, the same you would do for someone else, to allow space. Of course, when you don't see, you don't move away that two or three inches and quite often in my case, when we're both moving fast, the poor passerby nearly goes down like an NFL quarterback being hit by a 350-pound lineman. When they see your cane, they don't expect you to give that little extra space and some spectacular collisions are avoided (especially when the other person is counting aisles, and carrying popcorn, cokes, and four Red's tamales). After a brew or three, a buddy of mine once told me at a game; "Hey Roy, that's really trippy you have that blind stick. That lets everybody know you can eat everything with your fingers!" I don't feel using my long cane makes me stand out in a crowd. In fact, I'm never offended and actually honored when a pan handler hits me up for money, it makes me feel like I'm being treated like everyone else.

Again, since they just released me from the certifiable ward, I have another bit of advice that actually can be beneficial. Our two hands can be our best tools when we're losing our vision. Of course, touching things on a table or work area orients us and arranges things around us, but we also can use our hands in special ways, No, making questionable hand gestures to the cop that just gave your friend a ticket, isn't cool. With the snowballing advances in medicine, you never know, you may someday drive again and meet him up close and personal.

The outside of the hands from the tip of the little finger to the side of the palm and the area from the outside of the index finger to the "Devine Gate," the V between the index finger and thumb, is very sensitive, and can deflect projections that will catch or hang up on your fingers and fingertips as you search or touch things or flat areas to identify them. When you think about it, even if you have perfect vision, one of the most common results of reaching for things you can't see is catching a finger or thumb on the object's edge or top and over or down it goes. This is why you always, whenever possible, approach items from table or desk level. But the edge of the hand is a great soft touching tool for moving along inner or familiar outside walls and corridors. This term is "trailing," and once you are familiar with an area, you need only to touch the surface occasionally to orient your direction and route. These tactile techniques work simultaneously with something, something I keep losing on a daily basis: my mind. You would be amazed at how quickly your brain can memorize space and directionality when you don't see well. Jan and I have been blessed to now live in a large Mediterranean villa with many curved halls and wide, open areas. Quite often, I have walked through the lower floor and reached out and opened the handle of one of the doors leading out to the courtyard. The unusual thing about this is often I don't touch one thing from one side of the building to the other. These orientation skills aren't assimilated instantly, but over a period of time. This is another great example of how our mind adapts to changes in input and external sound and tactile body cues.

These tips and suggestions will be useful and the visually impaired person will soon adapt, but the most important things for you to impress on one who's losing their sight are: with the saturation of modern media, most of the population think of the blind as having special attributes, if you need help, don't ever be embarrassed to ask, keep up your skills and independence and remember one last thing, as you move forward through your life, you will occasionally need a little more space. Hey, why go through life as a Mini-Cooper when you can be a Madden-Cruiser bus.

67. Big Mama Ethyl— A Billion-To-One Chance

Finding something, or discovering a treasure you never expected, is always a joy, but this last story will surely evaporate any thoughts one might entertain that things only happen by sheer, dumb luck.

"Big Mama Ethyl"— saw her out of the corner of my ear. I guess she was the closest to a well-traveled and do-it-all girlfriend a guy could ever have. Lord knows she had a few years on her, and with a few imperfections, was certainly gaudy, and definitely a true dirty blond. Her classic shaped head was distinctive, recognizable clear across a crowded nightclub. To the few guys over the years lucky enough to caress it, her neck was too thick for modern taste, and her over-sized body was heavier than most, but it only made her warm voice richer and more resonant. But don't let Ethyl's size detract from your mental picture of her. Every curve was definitely in the right place. She was one of those playthings you couldn't leave alone for a single minute, for as soon as your back was turned, every other dude in the room who did the same things you did, wanted to get their hands on her to try and show you up. You had to pay attention to her all night long, because as temperamental as she was, the heat and chill always had an effect on her performance.

On many a late night, as soon as I had her right where I could feel the groove, she'd change right in the middle of my best effort. Over the years, hundreds of guys tried to take her away, some even offered enough money to make me think hard about letting her go, but there was no chance for them. Nobody could make her sing quite the same as me, and she always

214

made me give that little extra when she was in my lap. I knew every inch of her aging and artistic body, every quirk and flaw of her beautiful symmetry.

Now before you stop reading, thinking the teacher has suddenly reverted to cheap sex-riddled paperback clichés, let me explain. Ethyl is my 1936 Epiphone "Emperor" jazz guitar. There were not many of them built, and at the time she was conceived, she was one of the largest arch-top guitars ever constructed. The arch-top guitar has a curved face or soundboard and F-shaped holes on the carved top, very much like a cello or violin. Most of the acoustic guitars we see these days are the round-hole flat top style, used in country and pop music. I was told at the time I found Ethyl, she had belonged to Freddie Green, *Count Basie*'s guitarist for decades. One of my old band members had found a picture of Freddie playing a guitar exactly like Ethyl. Again, it's all relative, like saying "Paul Bunyan cut down half the trees in Minnesota using this big axe."

Soon after I bought her, I had one of the best guitar men on the West Coast put an electric pickup system on her so I could play her amplified with a band. He was able to do the installation without making a single hole in the instrument larger than a small screw. I've played this old guitar in every place imaginable for over 40 years, and I'd love to hear her stories of some of the things that happened around her in the years before me. She is still in mint condition and has her original case. Her value to a collector would be in the multi thousands of dollars. I'll never sell her unless I become totally destitute, and even then, maybe we'll just go on the road. Remember the words of an old Italian philosopher: "No matter how thin the soles of your shoes are getting, you're that much closer to having your feet back on the ground."

In the late 1980's, something happened that reinforced my belief in someone out there taking care of us. I rarely took Ethyl anywhere other than special gigs where I would be playing solo, where she was needed for jazz, or when I was doing a solo show where her fat and warm sound was required. Like so many other guitarists, I used the Les Paul or Fender Stratocaster solid-body rock guitar for most of my pop and rock gigs and kept Ethyl for the more sedate settings. One week, I was doing some recordings at a studio in Fremont and took her to school with me every day. Every night I'd pack her up and take her home on the BART train. About three days into the week, I went into the locked studio where I'd left her that morning, having decided to use her in a class I was about to teach. She was gone!

Minutes later I had called the Fremont Police, who immediately sent an officer out to take a report. I can't explain how sick I felt, angry with myself for not being more careful, and sicker at the thought that she was probably gone forever. I soon discovered I'd turned the new locking mechanism on the studio door the wrong way and had unlocked the door instead of locking it. The music building is very close to the outside access street and one of the bus stops for the school. Someone had either walked through the building while I was on recess duty that day or stolen her sometime that morning.

One of my friends was a detective with the Fremont Police Department, and he promised he'd do everything in his power to help me get her back. He was true to his word. For three weeks, he and other officers combed every avenue of where she might be: flea markets, pawn shops, swap meets, and even classified ads in all the local papers. In the same newspapers, the owner of the club where I was playing offered a thousand-dollar reward for her return. One of the Bay Area entertainment critics heard about my loss and helped get a front-page article printed in the local newspaper group. It covered six different cities and communities. While playing at my wife's restaurant at Jack London Square years earlier on a Halloween night, someone had taken a large photo of me with Ethyl. I was standing in front of the stage, dressed in a Keystone Cops uniform holding Ethyl by the neck, out to my side. I was pointing a nightstick at her and scowling, as if to say, "You're responsible for this dastardly deed." It was a fantastic shot of the guitar, and the papers used it in the article written by a Fremont journalist. In the story, I described how attached I'd become to the guitar, having traveled thousands of miles performing with her, and feeling as if I'd lost not only my sight, but also my right arm. I can truthfully say it was the only time in my life that I publicly mentioned my blindness as an "attention getter." Sadly, none of the wonderful people's efforts to help me were successful. In time, as the months passed, it became a dead issue.

Nearly a year later to the day, I received a phone call at the School for the Blind. When I answered, the young, soft voice of a woman spoke. She sounded no older than her late teens. She asked, "Is this Mr. Siligo?" When I said it was, she continued, "I think I might have your guitar." She began to describe the guitar she had, and my heart began to pound. It sounded just like Ethyl! But as she gave details of the guitar case, I thought I'd be physically sick, for it was nothing like the one that had held my guitar. The young woman said she and her husband, who was in the navy, were living in Vallejo, for he was stationed at Mare Island Submarine Base. I explained I'd have a difficult time getting up to where they lived and would be willing to pay them generously to bring the guitar to me, just to see if it could possibly be mine. She said they couldn't come until later that evening, after her husband got home from the base. I assured her I'd make it worth their time, and the next five hours seemed a decade. I had to play that night at the club, but there was no way I was moving from that spot until I found out for sure.

They drove up after six o'clock that evening, and a young man in his middle twenties got out of the car and introduced himself. I met his wife and held my breath as he took the guitar they'd brought out of the back of their van. The young man handed me the case, and my spirit dropped like an anvil. The handle was not the same, and even the smell of the case wasn't right. I laid the case down on the ground and felt the outside surface of it. Again, it was strange and rough, not at all the same. I felt the hinges to open it, and a spark began to burn in my gut. It felt right. Could it be another guitar of the same model, or one similar inside?

When I opened it, bells rang and rockets exploded in my brain. I would have recognized the smell of her spruce and birds-eye maple in a hurricane. I ran my fingers over her neck and body. As I took her out of the case, there was no longer any doubt it was Ethyl. All the familiar nicks and surface cracks were there, and to my amazement five of the six strings on her when she was stolen still remained. They were special compound wound jazz strings I'd been ordering from back East for years. A rough nickel wound string had replaced one that must've broken. I couldn't help it, but tears began running down my face, and I couldn't talk for a few minutes. I remember saying softly over and over again, "Oh God. Thank you, God."

You must think blind guys cry a lot and are perhaps overly emotional, and who knows, maybe in my case that's true. But it's almost impossible to convey to someone who isn't a musician, the bond and cohesiveness one forms with an inanimate object that has almost been a part of you for so many years. I practically pulled the young man's arm off shaking his hand, hugging and thanking him profusely, making a complete blubbering ass out of myself. I didn't care at that moment. I carried Ethyl into the music building, and had the young couple follow me as soon as the husband parked their vehicle. We sat down inside, and I explained what had happened a year ago, and showed them the very room from where Ethyl had been stolen.

His wife began to tell me how the events had unfolded. A year earlier, she'd been sitting in a beauty salon in Vallejo waiting to have her hair done. She was nearly sixty miles from the school in Fremont. A stocky young man came in carrying some things. Among them was a large guitar case. He told the women sitting around the room that he had to sell some of his and his wife's things to raise rent money, or they were going to be evicted the following week. He had some jewelry, a woman's watch, and some leather goods. The sailor's wife said her husband was just learning some chords on the guitar, and the one the man was selling looked old, but beautiful. She had no idea of its value and told the thief she could only come up with two hundred fifty dollars cash, for she'd just gone to the bank for some money for a birthday party for her husband that Sunday. The thief grumbled about the amount, but took the money, leaving the guitar behind. The husband told his wife (when she gave it to him as a birthday present) that it looked very expensive, but he didn't know for sure because he'd never seen a guitar like that up close. He knew a fellow at the base who had an Epiphone flat top guitar, and it had cost him nearly four hundred bucks. Of course, the young sailor didn't know the name Epiphone had been sold many times over the years, and since the 1970's the guitars were made in Korea and Japan. Ethyl, built by the original company, was hand crafted in New York. Soon after the birthday party, the young sailor went east for a six-month navy submarine repair school. The couple took Ethyl with them. Before coming back to the San Francisco Bay Area, they traveled down the East Coast all the way to Florida and across the Southern states, stopping for several days at various campgrounds. They'd only been back in Vallejo for a couple of months.

"How did you find out the guitar was mine?" I asked. What follows is the strangest and most amazing part of this story. The young woman had been visiting her mother who lived in the town of Livermore, just on the other side of the mountains from the School for the Blind where Ethyl was stolen. The young lady was about to set the dining room table for Thanksgiving dinner (her husband was to join them later that evening) when she found a folded piece of newsprint with the napkins and tablecloths in the top drawer of her mom's buffet. She opened up the article and saw the picture of the very same guitar she'd given her husband. In astonishment, she read the story and then asked her mother what the piece from the paper was doing in her drawer. Her mother told her the story had moved her so much when she read it nearly a year earlier, she'd cut it out and saved it. The daughter had gotten my name from the news story.

Often today, as I play that wonderful old instrument, I think of the astronomically slim chance that anyone would clip and save such a story, and after traveling all over the U.S., someone else would find the article and actually have the subject of it in their possession. What had thrown me off when the young woman described Ethyl's case on the phone was the fact that the thief had disguised it by changing the handle and wrapping it in black vinyl strips. All over the lid and back of the case were large bumper stickers saying, "Chevy Goes," "Harley Davidson," and a dozen other modern slogans, all of which must've offended "Big Mama Ethyl" to no end! Who knows, maybe it made her feel a little younger.

With my eyes still cloudy, I went into a closet in my main music room. I took a beautiful early-sixties vintage Martin D18 acoustic guitar from inside. I'd purchased it over ten years earlier to play Hawaiian slack key guitar. At the time I bought it, it was worth well over two grand. I took it to the young sailor and said it was his, as a thank you for bringing Ethyl home. After I opened the case and showed it to him, he took it almost reluctantly. I heard the smile in his thank you, like a kid on Christmas morning. He shook my hand again, and his wife gave me a hug before climbing into their van. I tried to give them a couple of twenties for gas, but they refused. When she hugged me, I noticed she was at least seven months pregnant. I stood at the curb of the traffic circle outside the school for a very long time after they left, thinking of what wonderful young people live in this country, and how fortunate that I'd seen them and experienced their honesty and grace firsthand. Simple acts such as theirs seem to find precious little space in the negative-charged rooms of our mass media mansions, overshadowed by "bigger," more sensational issues. I believe we all should realize that basic goodness and caring is and always will be all around us, if we just take the time to notice.

We all realize the events and tensions in these first decades of this new century will change history. But I believe each of us still has a voice and an impact on the overall picture. Sometimes our "selfness" clouds the picture a bit but reaching out to our neighbors and friends soon pulls the image back into focus. Often many of us, with or without disabilities, become too involved in our own unique and sometimes self-defeating personal attitudes. Some of us spend far too much energy and thought in balancing the chips on our shoulders, while keeping the insecurity inside us at bay. Until someone or something comes along and shakes our tree, we sometimes fail to remember that one of life's greatest gifts is the ability to laugh at ourselves. Our lives would be so much richer if all of us could accept our imperfections and those of others, appreciate and respect who we truly are, and give less importance to how we think we must be seen through others' eyes. If this much of my journey has taught me one thing, it is that people, and our daily interactions with each other, are the life pulse of being alive. Though we may not always succeed, as long as we reach out and try to make someone's life a little richer, the effort is rewarded both from within us, and from those we touch daily.

I can only offer my thoughts from my heart and past experiences, but I rest in the knowledge that they are honest. No matter who we are, every once in a while, (as in my case) we win big-time. But when life jumps up and bites us on the butt, we must remember that with all the supporting cast around us, we're guaranteed it will still be a great show.

Made in the USA
Las Vegas, NV
06 March 2022